The New

LOVING RELATIONSHIPS

Book

The New

LOVING RELATIONSHIPS

Book

SONDRA RAY

with MARKUS RAY

Immortal Ray Productions
Nashville   Washington D.C.

Immortal Ray Productions
301 Tingey Street SE
Washington D.C. 20003
immortalrayproductions@gmail.com
www.sondraray.com

Immortal Ray Productions
Nashville   Washington D.C.

ISBN 978-1-54260-416-1 (paperback)
ASIN: B06VWWY39H (e-book)

Ordering Information:
Quantity sales. Special discounts are available on quantity purchases by corporations, associations, and others. For details, "Contact Us" at the address above.

Photos of Sondra Ray & Markus Ray on cover by Judy Totton of London
Photo of Sondra Ray & Markus Ray on page iii by John Bonath of Denver
Painting of Quan Yin on page xxiii by Markus Ray

OTHER BOOKS
BY SONDRA RAY

- ❖ Rebirthing in the New Age
- ❖ I Deserve Love
- ❖ Loving Relationships I
- ❖ The Only Diet There Is
- ❖ Celebration of Breath
- ❖ Ideal Birth
- ❖ Drinking the Divine
- ❖ Pure Joy
- ❖ Inner Communion
- ❖ How To Be Chic, Fabulous and Live Forever
- ❖ Interlude With the Gods
- ❖ Loving Relationships II
- ❖ Essays on Creating Sacred Relationships
- ❖ Healing and Holiness
- ❖ Pele's Wish
- ❖ Relationships Treasury
- ❖ Rock Your World with the Divine Mother
- ❖ Liberation Breathing: The Divine Mother's Gift
- ❖ Spiritual intimacy: What You Really Want With a Mate
- ❖ Babaji: My Miraculous Meetings With A Maha Avatar

Books By Markus Ray

- ❖ Liberation Breathing: The Divine Mother's Gift
- ❖ Odes to the Divine Mother
- ❖ Miracles With My Master, Tara Singh
- ❖ Babaji: My Miraculous Meetings With A Maha Avatar

Contents

DEDICATION

I dedicate this book to Shri Shri 1008 Shri Bhagwan Herakhan Wale Baba, The Yogi Christ of India, who teaches me what I need to know, who helps me teach what I know, who guides me eternally, and who gives me this supremely wonderful, most important relationship.

Om Namaha Shivai

May everything I write be something beautiful for God.

THE REASON THIS BOOK IS DIFFERENT from other books you may have read on relationships is because it is based on the following:

1. The spiritual truth that *thought is creative* and that you can change anything by changing your thoughts; you can especially change the deep subconscious thoughts that are destructive to relationships;

2. New research from the effects of Birth Trauma. This information was never available before. Liberation Breathinig/Rebirthing, a process that heals the damage done physically and psychologically at birth, came about over forty years ago and has clearly taught us how your birth affects your relationships;

3. The concept of Physical Immortality — learning how to master your body so that you can start *youthing* and keep your body any age you wish. This means you can prolong your life as long as you like once you master the philosophy, continue Breathwork, and change your thoughts.

Because of these spiritual truths and the fact that we are now entering the true age of enlightenment, ours may be the first generation in which relationships work in such a way that they bring us total healing and aliveness.

"The only way to have a perfect relationship is to have two people both willing to experience their own perfection."

—Leonard Orr—

FOREWORD

A ROSE BY ANY OTHER NAME

I have been on a 30+ year journey with Sondra Ray. Somewhere back in 1986, I met her at a *Loving Relationships Training* in Philadelphia. When she told me the absolute truth—that "your thoughts create your results" in all experiences—my eyes were opened. I had been to college twice by then, held a Master's degree, and no one ever put such a clear and simple truth in front of me. This one statement transformed my life. Sondra Ray continues to inspire and transform my life, and now she is my wife.

On August 31, 2016, I legally changed my name to Markus Ray. On that day, I put both feet into my divine destiny to be the twin flame and consort of Sondra Ray. I affirmed not only to the universe, but also to the legal "powers that be," that I am who I am—Markus Ray. I am who I am as God created me, and I am co-creating with Sondra Ray, along with the great Life Source of the Cosmos, to be Markus Ray. I am assigning this name with God to the rose of my true Self, which by any other name would still be that sweet-smelling rose. With Sondra Ray, I ascend into the unlimited possibilities of my soul, and leave behind the limitations that I once believed was "me."

Years ago, I heard Bod Dylan answer a question when someone asked him about changing his name to Bob Dylan from Robert Zimmerman. He looked at the interviewer like the question was absolutely absurd, and said, "Man, you can be anybody you want to be." He was clear that his new name *Bob Dylan* had all the vibration and all the force that would define his "rose" better than his old name did. It was a "no brainer" to him—quite obvious. He was a poet, and he had to have a name that was commensurate with that divine destiny of being who he ascended into, as God created him. I never forgot this exchange. I never forgot his answer.

It was easy for me to make this decision to change my name. I was entering into holy relationship with a *goddess*, and taking her name would lift me into higher dimensions. Marianne Williamson wrote this of Sondra Ray:

> *"If Sondra Ray writes a new book, I read it. I let go of my left-brain and drink her in, imagining her sitting on a chair, explaining to me what to her was so obvious and to*

the rest of us, well, maybe not so much. I have never experienced Sondra as anything other than a beam of light, either streaming at me from the page of a book or through the wondrous woman with a flower behind her ear. I have lived enough to be able to say that of all the good fortunes I have had in my life, encountering her has been one of the loveliest. Sondra Ray is more than a woman. The word goddess comes to mind."

Before my marriage with Sondra Ray, her divine destiny had already been set. This is her history: author, lecturer, spiritual mentor, visionary, new-age pioneer, world-teacher. These were just a few aspects of the multifaceted richness of Sondra Ray's illustrious past and present. For her to take my last name would have been ludicrous, so a new precedent was needed—a new way for two people to enter into a holy union. We both wanted a solution that invoked not only the divine masculine of "God the Father," but also the divine feminine of "God the Mother." I was inspired when I saw the possibility of changing my name to *Markus Ray*. Why not? From an epiphany in a rebirthing session in 2012, I became Markus Ray.

The "legalities" of that name change took more effort. Sondra Ray and I were actually married in India at Babaji's ashram on April 4th, 2009. Muniraj, one of our spiritual masters, said, "Where truth is spoken no papers are necessary." We did not think that we should be concerned with the *legalities* of that union. But when I would always have to affirm my old name on legal papers—such as passports, bank accounts, and driver's licenses—I felt the switch to *Markus Ray* was only "half done." So in mid-August of 2016 I started the legal process and filed for a name change at the Nashville, Tennessee courthouse. A hearing was set for September 1st.

We actually arrived a day early, and were the last ones in the courtroom waiting for our turn before the judge. He looked at his docket, then he looked at me and said, "Today is August 31st, you are a day early." Again, I felt my heart sink. "But you have come all this way," he encouraged, "I think we can work you in." The judge found my paperwork and looked it over with an eagle's eye. "You don't have a birth certificate here," he pointed out. I acknowledged that fact, hanging on the edge, expecting him to throw out my case. "But you have other documentation that looks good." Then there was a long pause. I was rubbing my little brass pocket Ganesh, the *remover of obstacles*, secretly in my pants pocket. Then with a robust voice of authority, Judge Randy Kennedy of the 7th Circuit Court of the State of Tennessee said, "I now declare you Markus Ray."

This was a moment of destiny that had taken 30 years to play out. When I met Sondra Ray in the summer of 1986 I had no idea what a journey it would be. This is what Love does. It grabs your heart and takes you on a ride that you never expected. It takes you to regions of truth and beauty that you cannot find on your own. It puts you in new dimensions of Life that may have similar parts and familiar necessities, but rearranges them in a totally new configuration that merges with the destiny and mystery of the Cosmos.

Judge Kennedy said one more thing, "You are really on the cutting edge of a new precedent, taking your wife's name." That, I was. Perhaps this is part of the answer in these times—one man is surrendering to the Divine Mother and saying the patriarchal models are not working. On that day I declared I am Markus Ray, one who has surrendered to the Divine Feminine Energy of Creation, to the Divine Mother of all things, and to Sondra Ray who represents Her.

Sondra Ray created a roadmap for relationships in 1975 when she began teaching *The Loving Relationships Training, The LRT®,* around the world. In 1980, she wrote the book *Loving Relationships* that unlocked the doors for thousands of people who wanted to get clear on why their relationships were the way they were. And it gave them the tools to do something about them. No longer could people languish in the familiar dysfunctional patterns of their parents without questioning the possibility of another way. Sondra Ray took this to be her *life's work,* helping to awaken you and me to a higher and more loving frequency for our relationships. I venture to say she succeeded in this mission, and continues wisely to this day—still in it.

Back then people were very unclear that their family patterns and negative subconscious beliefs had such a tenacious hold on the health of their relationships. Even the preverbal thoughts people formed from their "birth trauma" affected their relationships. These "thoughts" were the principle causes for their life's effects, for better or worse. Most were caught in the repetitive unconscious memories of the past, full of conflicts and tendencies of the *family mind*, and just put up with the rumblings of discontent that seemed to underlie almost all relationships.

Well, people are still not very clear today about the "cause and effects" of their thoughts, and the blocks these deep seeded family patterns and habits pose to having loving, peaceful and lasting relationships. This is why Sondra Ray and I have revived this classic work, *Loving Relationships*. Our mission in the 21st century is to awaken people to new ways of thinking about relationships—to achieve deeper connection, to communicate more truthfully, to be intimate spiritually as well as emotionally, and to make new connections to our Source energy that make our relationships truly more *loving*, right now. You don't have to wait. You can easily read and apply what is in *The New Loving Relationships Book* to all your relationships *NOW*.

A rose by any other name would smell just as sweet. May *The New Loving Relationships Book* help you step into the inspiration of your divine destiny. May it be a beacon of hope and transformation for you who are searching for a higher truth within yourself. May Sondra Ray's words, from that Source energy Marianne Williamson suggested comes from nothing short of a *goddess*, uplift and enlighten you. May this book aid you on your journey to discover that your real name is Love, and that rose of your true Self, by any other name, in all of your relationships will smell just as sweet.

—**Markus Ray**—

Washington D.C.

ACKNOWLEDGEMENT

August 24, 2016

The Reason I Love Sondra Ray.

- Today is my wife, Sondra Ray's birthday. She is eternally young as an Immortalist, so we do not do "age" in our household. She is in the present for me, ageless—and the joie de vivre she had when I met her in 1986 is the same unquenchable PURE JOY she has right now, in every moment.

- The reason I Love my wife the most is that she always tells the truth. When I get "off," she sets me back on track, directly but gently. She helps all the people we meet see the truth as well, and that is always dynamic and fun.

- The reason I Love my wife, Sondra Ray, is that she always goes outside the "thoughts of limitation," and suggests something outrageous that is more alive, more creative, more of the "impossible" made possible.

- The reason I Love my wife is that she is a great lover in all areas of our life, and that includes the sensual area of our life as well.

- The reason I absolutely Love my wife is because we have Spiritual Intimacy and relate to the Masters directly, Babaji, Jesus of A Course in Miracles, and the Divine Mother. With her there is no "middle man." We go directly to the Source.

- The reason I love my wife is that she is so open-minded, and reads voraciously others' ideas and writings, and is in a constant state of wonder, of curiosity, and therefore increasing her awareness and sensitivity.

- The reason I Love my wife so much is she takes me so much higher in my life than I could go myself without her.

- The reason I Love my wife so passionately is that she Loves God above all else, and then she transfers that Love to me. And I reap the benefits.

- The reason I love my wife so immensely is that she goes beyond all reasons to Love, and puts me in the frequency of Immortality in which Ascension and

Liberation are not only possible for me in this lifetime, but inevitable.

- Sondra Ray, You are my everything. Happy Birthday!

—Markus Ray—
Facebook Post, 24-AUG-2016

INTRODUCTION

Since I originally wrote this book, my whole life has changed dramatically. I benefited so much from this material that I was able to meet my twin flame, Markus. We have been married eight years now and we are together 24/7/365 living in harmony precisely because we applied what is in this book. I experience sheer happiness being with this wonderful man. He and I have also taken Rebirthing to a new expression, which to me is a lot more spiritual because we work with the Divine Mother energy in the sessions. Hence, we call this work Liberation Breathing®, a new expression of Rebirthing. Our goal is to help people be liberated from all suffering.

The first edition of this book was very popular, so I decided to revive it. It has been a joy to re-write it. It starts with the simple things and develops into the more advanced subjects. In the end, I totally revamped the entire book. I have learned so much since I first wrote *Loving Relationships* in 1980, I have ended up writing a whole new book—really. It is a manual that applies to everybody, because life is all about relationships, and everybody is in them. Even if you are single and living alone, you still have a relationship with your Self and your Creator. I have renamed it, simply:

The New
LOVING RELATIONSHIPS
Book

Prior to writing the first edition of *Loving Relationships*, I created The Loving Relationships Training, (The LRT®.) Back then there were no seminars on this important life subject. I created it from my research I had done from all my Rebirthing clients who came to me with issues in relationships. I created it so that you can fully love yourself and experience an abundance of love and joy in all your relationships—all of the time. It remains one of the best weekend seminars Markus and I teach. This book contains many ideas from the training and is intended to help you heal yourself in your present relationships and to clear your mind right now on the whole subject of relationships.

Would you rather know how to prevent dramas and

traumas in your relationships, ahead of time, or would you rather just throw yourself in and see what happens? Most people do the latter. I tell you it is much less painful to have the information in this book to guide you. Why not have it easier? Most people are just re-running the wounds of their childhood in relationships. Most people get in a relationship without having any idea how to solve the problem of conflicts that are bound to come up. I can tell you it is a lot more fun if you know techniques that are guaranteed to resolve conflicts. I can tell you it is a lot more fun to know how to prevent fights. I can tell you that it is a lot more fun to learn how to have a conflict free relationship. Most people think it is not possible but I can tell you it is. The answers are in this book.

This book is about letting go of all your past negative ideas about relationship. This book is a guide to having sane, fun relationships. This book is about handling all the issues that can come up in any relationship. It is important because it covers things that other books on this subject never cover such as 1) How your birth trauma affects relationships 2) How your preverbal thoughts affect relationships 3) How your death urge affects relationships. This is relevant to everyone in all cases.

The original book, *Loving Relationships*, was read by many who came back to me decades later and said, "That book really changed my life," so I know this works. At the time, in the 70's and 80's, I was one of the few people who had the nerve to teach a weekend seminar on relationships. People were so grateful to have any knowledge on the subject back then—so I was a real novelty. I am sure you can imagine how much more I have learned in the last two-and-a-half decades. That is why I just rewrote the whole thing, improving it for these times. And now I am in a loving relationship with my husband, Markus. Back then I was not. Now, we have applied all the principles in this book to find out they actually work. He has also made some important contributions throughout.

Some of the material that gives real solutions is the same. But I have been able to elaborate on those solutions in a much deeper way now. There are solutions for how to find a mate. There are solutions on how to handle a new relationship after the person shows up. There are solutions how to prevent arguments. There are solutions how to communicate well in a relationship. There are solutions how to keep your relationship "cleaned up". There are solutions to change difficult situations. There are solutions for how to determine if you should stay in a difficult relationship or if you should leave. There are solutions how to have peace and happiness in your life in general and in your relationship.

There is a new chapter on "Giving Up Anger." In our trainings we teach worldwide, this is one of the most difficult sections to teach, but also the most liberating. In many cultures around the world we find the same attachment to anger, and people try to *justify* it. Well, Jesus in *A Course in Miracles* says, "Anger is never justified, " and He means *never. (ACIM; Text; Chapter 30; Section vi)* He goes on to make the case for complete forgiveness, in which peace and joy are restored.

It is my intention that you enjoy reading this book. I am very confident you will love it. People loved it before in the first edition, and this edition is much better—so I know you will love more, even now. I am convinced it is one of the best books to read on the subject because it covers points that I have never read in other books on relationships. I recommend you even try reading it out loud to your partner. ENJOY!!

— SONDRA RAY —

L THE ♥RT®

1. HOW I CREATED THE LOVING RELATIONSHIP TRAINING

The Loving Relationship Training is pure pleasure to me—it has never been work. Everyone wants to know how I created the LRT. Well, when I went to California in the 70's I needed to find a seminar on relationships for myself; but I could not find one. I asked people, "Where is there training on relationships?" The answer I got was funny. They said, "Everyone is too screwed up in that area to teach it!" Well, I thought, "Someone should do it—does it have to be me?" Then I read a study that blew my mind. It was from the Mayo Clinic in Minnesota. It was a study done on average Americans in the 1980s. It dealt with the stages of relationships.

SONDRA RAY & MARKUS RAY

- ❖ The first stage was called "The Dream Stage." This, they said, only lasts for two months on the average.
- ❖ The next stage was called "The Disillusionment Stage." That is when you find out all those things you don't like about this mate. This could go on for two years!
- ❖ The next stage was called "The Misery Stage." This describes the couple after many years of marriage, children, with some negative relationship issues and no time or way to clear them. One or both may end up drinking too much, getting fat, gambling, getting sick, and having an affair or whatever. That makes it worse. This stage, they said, could go on for thirty years! That was a shocker.
- ❖ The next stage was called the "Enlightenment Stage." This is when the couple stops blaming each other and begins to look at themselves.
- ❖ The final stage was called "Mutual Respect."

My problem with this study was that by the time you get to the last two stages you are too old to enjoy them.

I really, really wanted to know how I could jump from the dream stage to the enlightenment stage and skip thirty years of misery. So, I became really interested in this topic. Furthermore, my clients in breathwork came to me and told me all about their problems in relationships. I would give them a session and they would have a memory of their birth

2

and I could see how their birth trauma was affecting their relationships. So I had all this data and research in my head.

When I first began sharing it, people were amazed to no end and they would say things like, "Sondra this explains everything." They would bring all their friends to hear me and their friends had the same reaction. They all told me it was too powerful for a one-day session, and I needed to teach it in two days. So then I started writing the training in a two-day format. Now I have it is a three-day format.

I also have to admit that my own birth affected my curiosity about relationships. My midwife was my father's high school sweetheart. She wanted him to come home from college and marry her. Instead he went to college and met this Swedish woman (my mother). My mother knew about this other woman and decided the best thing would be to become her best friend. So this woman (Verna) was even attending my birth assisting the doctor. However, at my birth she got insanely jealous and wanted me to be her baby. She then wanted to give me a different name so she and my mom argued over that. My father flipped out and went outside on the porch to have a cigarette. This screwed up my birth because then I stopped coming out and waited for my father to come back. He didn't. So then the doctor started pulling on my head and I had an injury about my sinuses. I was aware of all this and was more or less saying from inside: "Would you all please get clear on your relationships so I can come out?"

Later I was fascinated with everyone's relationships in my town; the population was only three hundred so I knew everything about everyone. You might say I was interested in this topic my whole life. It became my destiny.

When I started out, I certainly was not clear on everything. You can never know everything on this topic. But I succeeded because I had the nerve to stand up and teach what I knew and I always told the truth about what I did not know. I am still learning and people who shared in the training taught me so much. And of course, my clients in Liberation Breathing/Rebirthing taught me heaps. I am still learning more day by day.

In the beginning, I did the training on Friday night, all day Saturday and all day Sunday. Then, I would have a group LB/Rebirthing session Monday night. But then people started going in spontaneous rebirthing sessions during the training. So, I started doing one breathwork session on Sunday night during the training. Then people requested a breathwork session Saturday night. Then they requested one Friday night. Now we do a breathwork session every day. That way nobody is sitting in his or her chair suffering with discomfort. Breathwork helps people integrate the shifts in their minds brought forth from the new mindset on relationships that the LRT is so good at presenting.

When I started going to India and met Babaji, my life changed and I became much more powerful. The LRT certainly went to a new level because I did. People began to experience more and more miracles in the training. It was amazing. When my mother died, I had to take a long break to recover, so things sort of died out because my death urge was activated. When I recovered from all that (see my book *Healing and Holiness*,) I had to start over. Finally, when my wonderful husband came into my life, I gained all kinds of new insights and re-wrote the training in a better way. We tried it out in Italy. A very famous British man who had been knighted by the Queen was in the training. He said to me afterwards: "This training has changed my whole life—it is a crime if you don't start doing it everywhere again." So I did. Now we have the new improved LRT and I am as excited to do it in this new millennium, as I always was.

2. MEETING AND MATING

The soul draws toward itself the circumstances and people it needs for its highest development. In the same way, our karma and vibrational patterns draw to us the very person we need to help us grow.

It is very easy to attract a mate or anyone if you think that you can! If you understand a little metaphysics, the days of worrying and hoping and looking in singles bars are over. There is such a thing as the "Universal Metaphysical Law of Attraction." I prefer to call it *The Cosmic Dating Service.* It always works too, if you let it. You don't have to worry about the where or the how. The person you are looking for will show up *anywhere,* when and only when you are ready. You merely have to think the right thoughts and let go of any resistance you have to receiving. So what you do is tell God what you want. You ask and it is given. But you have to allow it to happen. Then you can say to God, "If I am not ready, make me ready."

The mistake that most people make is forgetting that their thoughts produce results *all the time*—especially their sub-conscious thoughts. People walk around thinking things like, "I'll never find anybody," or, "There aren't any available men (or women) around here," or, "Nobody ever asks me out," and then they wonder why they are home alone! Especially after there is a breakup, the person "left behind" usually ends up thinking something like, "I'll never find anyone as good as him (or her)," or "I'll never make it alone," or "My life is over." All of these thoughts are destructive and produce negative results.

It is important to keep your heart open to receive. Then, it is a matter of accepting and being certain that you deserve what you want. A good affirmation is, "I am so happy and grateful that my perfect mate is here now." If you do not get a result after saying and writing this affirmation for a period of time, then you have a block—or what I call a "counter-intention." You have a sabotaging thought buried somewhere and you must find it. This can be discovered and released easily by using the affirmation technique this book describes and especially by getting a Liberation Breathing or Rebirthing/Breathwork session.

You will tend to attract mates who fit into your family

patterns until you clear them. After you understand and become cleared of those patterns, you will automatically attract someone who is in harmony with your highest thoughts, and then life will be easy. The best way to clear out old "neurotic" family patterns is through Liberation Breathing (a breathing process that clears your consciousness way back to birth) and through the processes in the Loving Relationships Training. Meanwhile, this book is a good way to get started.

3. CLEARING UP YOUR RELATIONSHIP WITH GOD

Having a good relationship with Life itself is crucial to having a good relationship with another person. When you get really clear on your relationship with Life, everything starts working. To me God and the Life Force are one. In this work, we use *A Course in Miracles* as the foundation. *A Course in Miracles* is a correction of religion. It is Christian in tone because Christianity is a major influence on the planet and has to be corrected first. *A Course in Miracles* cleared me on all the things I was confused about due to my religious upbringing.

I needed help because I was angry at God for my father's death. That was because I was told as a child in Sunday school that when people died, "The Lord took them away." When I asked my Sunday school teacher one day, "Does that mean God kills people?" my teacher could not answer me. I was so confused by the time I got to my college years that the first time around I married an atheist. So that marriage was doomed. When I became conscious and straightened out my mind on spiritual matters, I started having good relationships. Now I teach *A Course in Miracles* to students, and I am married to a man who also teaches it. Wow! What a difference!

We don't try to define God but there are some things to know about how God works with your thoughts. God is the Great Affirmative that always says "Yes" to your thoughts; God is *energy* added to your thoughts. If I have a secret belief in my subconscious, "I am going to die when I am around seventy," God says, "Yes, whatever you say. You have free will," and gives more energy to that thought. When we become clear that thought is creative, we can say, "I am giving up the thought that death is inevitable and I am *youthing.*" God will add energy to that *thought.*

As soon as we know that we have all of God's power available to us—as much as we can take—then everything changes. We can love God! We don't have to fear surrendering to God, because we know that God does not *kill us.*

The truth is that you are the Source, and part of the Source. In other words, you and the Source are inseparable. All your relationships are up to you; you can have them however you want them because God the Source pours energy into your thoughts and desires. To me it is imperative that you are in a good relationship with the Source so you can have a Holy Relationship. What that is will be explained later in this book.

4. **GETTING ENLIGHTENED**

What if one mate understands how the mind works and the other does not? You are in for trouble if that is your case. Once I had a female client who was a lawyer and she was married to a lawyer. During her first Liberation Breathing session, she was able to heal a long-standing pain in the shoulder. She was excited about that and she committed to doing ten sessions with me. The more sessions she had the deeper she became spiritually. She was bothered because she could not share these changes with her husband. He was not interested. She got more and more bored with her marriage. So I asked her what she wanted to do. She said, "I want to leave." So I told her that I would help her get strong enough to do that. She would go home after the session and chicken out. She could not get the courage. This went on for eight sessions. Finally, I said to her, "You are not going to leave that marriage—so put your foot back in the door and make it work." Suddenly she started screaming, "I will die if I stay in that marriage."

So then I said, "Well, make up your mind because I am not willing to go through eight more sessions like this." Later she begged me to give him a session. I sensed he did not really want it. "If he comes to please you, it is not going to work," I told her. "He has to want it for himself." Anyway, I liked her so much that I decided to try it. He came to my apartment dressed in an expensive suit, starched shirt and tie—hardly what is appropriate for a breathing session. Anyway, l sat with him and at one point, I said, "I want to make sure you know that your thoughts create your results."

He said, "I don't believe that!" I said, "Sir, right here is where your marriage is stuck." He had a pretty good session but of course he decided he did not need *that*. He was unwilling to keep looking at himself. So then, she divorced him.

How can you clean up anything in a relationship unless you both understand this truth and how the mind works?

Leonard Orr, founder of Rebirthing used to say you cannot be enlightened unless you understand the Absolute Truth. The Absolute Truth is something that is true in all time and space, for everyone, equally, forever. The following should have been taught to us the first day of school. What is the Absolute Truth that leads to enlightenment?

- ❖ *The absolute truth is that thought is creative* — or
- ❖ *The thinker is creative with his thoughts.* (Any objection to the truth would be something you thought, which only goes to prove its validity.)
- ❖ *The thinker creates with his thoughts* — therefore
- ❖ *Thoughts produce results* — therefore
- ❖ *Your negative thoughts produce negative results for you* — and
- ❖ *Your positive thoughts produce positive results for you* — God is Energy added to your thoughts, and always says, "Yes," to you — therefore
- ❖ *What you think about expands* — and
- ❖ *What you think about you get more of.*

Your thoughts produce results even though you are no longer consciously thinking them. If something terrible happens to you, you might have trouble taking responsibility for creating it if you are not in touch with the deeply buried negative thought that originally created the situation. That is why it is so important to bring up and clear out those buried negative thoughts. Most people now days are aware that their thoughts create results, but what they forget it this: subconscious thoughts that you are not aware of are producing results also! We end up sabotaging our results because we are not aware of those suppressed thoughts. That is why we need something like Liberation Breathing or Rebirthing/Breathwork to bring up and cleanse those thoughts. We even study pre-verbal thoughts and how they affect a person. That is really our specialty.

An example of a pre-verbal thought or a thought from birth that can mess up relationships is one which many women accepted the moment they were hung upside down and hit on the bottom by a male obstetrician: "Men hurt me." Since the thinker is creative with his or her thoughts, this thought begins to produce results very early for a little girl. In kindergarten boys act out her beliefs by knocking her down or hitting her. She is teased by boys in grade school. Then in high school she starts dating and finds herself jilted because she still has the thought in her subconscious.

After a childhood and teenage of creating abuse from boys, she enters adulthood certain that men will hurt her. When a man comes along who seems to be nonthreatening, she lays aside her anxieties and recovers long enough to fall in love and get married. When that doesn't work out and her husband runs off with her best friend, the old belief that "men hurt me" is reinforced and she resolves to have nothing further to do with men. All the time, the males in her life were simply acting out her lifelong subconscious belief. She herself, of course, was not even conscious of it.

Obviously, women act out men's thoughts in the same way. A thought originating at birth for many men is that,

"Women want to suffocate (kill) me." Women may act this out by being too maternal and overprotective. Men usually interpret this as a sign that the women are trying to trap them. And so it goes. Thoughts create results.

The way to rid ourselves of these destructive subconscious thoughts is to repeat affirmations like these:

- ❖ I forgive the doctor for the pain he caused me at birth.
- ❖ I forgive my mother for the pain she caused me at birth.
- ❖ I forgive myself for the pain I caused myself at birth.
- ❖ Other men are not my obstetrician, or my father.
- ❖ Other women are not my mothers.

If you are totally familiar with how to use affirmations, you could skip the following chapter. Even so, you may benefit from reading this section.

5. USING AFFIRMATIONS

All thoughts are "affirmations"—even your negative ones. The mind is the ruler of your experience; therefore, your thoughts are always producing results. So why not be ruler of your mind, which means having dominion over your thoughts, which determine how you feel, and what you manifest in your experiences? There are many thoughts in your subconscious mind you are not even aware you have. Thank goodness! Could you imagine being aware of all the thoughts needed to run your involuntary body systems? What if you forgot to think about your heart beating, or your breathing during sleep? We are not concerned with those thoughts. But we are concerned with the thoughts that produce your painful and negative experiences.

The Affirmations we are discussing here are conscious thoughts that replace the negative ones you have. Why not start to process yourself on these negative thoughts? It is like being the Sherlock Holmes of your mind, often backtracking your mental "clues" that are the culprits of any undesirable outcomes. You can start with any experience or condition and say to yourself, "The negative thought that caused this experience is _____." Fill in the blank. Then do it again. "Another negative thought I have that caused this condition is _____." By applying this process, you will find the causative factors in your mind that need to be transmuted and released.

For example, if you were induced at your birth, you may have formed a thought, "I am not ready to come out." You may find yourself procrastinating because you often feel not ready to come out and be proactive. You may feel "others" are dictating the conditions for your moving forward. You may feel held back from having your own initiative. Or, you may overcompensate and have the thought, "I have to do everything myself." These thoughts are affecting your life until you change them. These are affirmations that correct those limiting thoughts.

❖ "I forgive myself for needing to be induced in this lifetime."

❖ "I forgive my delivery team for not letting me decide

when I wanted to come out."

❖ "I am now ready to come out on my own, and initiate my own actions."

❖ "I can start things easily and effortlessly, and complete them in good timing."

❖ "I can accept the help I need to support me with what I am doing."

❖ "I attract the right help to make major transitions in my life."

Betsy is typical of my many clients who have a very deep negative thought that nobody likes her or wants her. She was walking around with the thought in her subconscious, "Nobody likes me, nobody wants me," and then she was wondering why her relationships never worked. Before she got enlightened she was helpless to do anything about this. A man would come along and try to love her. She could not compute this because it was against her basic belief about herself. She was putting out psychically to men a kind of command that went, "Don't like me, don't want me." And so men responded to that telepathically and they didn't like or want her.

At first it was very hard for Betsy to believe that simply by changing her thoughts she could get a new result. I could empathize with her because I was once unable to believe it could be easy. She resisted doing the affirmation,

"Everybody likes me," because she said it was a lie. I explained to her that at first it will seem like a lie but she has to convince herself that it is not. I took her through it in stages. I had her write the following:

"Since I was the thinker that thought that nobody likes me and nobody wants me, I am also the thinker that can now think that people are starting to like me." After she accepted the new thought, "People are starting to like me," she began to notice a few changes. People responded to her differently. Once some people responded to her differently, she was able to convince herself, and she was able to shift to the thought, "People like me."

One has to re-program the mind as she did. It works. To help change a long-held negative thought, take a deep breath, pull in the new thought on the inhale and let go of the old thought on the exhale. This is a definition of an affirmation that I like:

An affirmation is a positive thought that you consciously choose to immerse in your consciousness to produce a certain desired result.

In other words, you give your mind an idea on purpose. Your mind will certainly create whatever you want if you give it a chance. By repetition, you can feed your mind positive thoughts and achieve your desired goal. There are various ways to use affirmations.

Probably the simplest and most effective way that I have found is to write each affirmation ten or twenty times on a sheet of paper, leaving a space in the right-hand margin of the page for emotional "responses." As the affirmation is written on the left side of the page, you also jot down whatever thoughts, considerations, beliefs, fears, or emotions that may come into your mind on the right side of the page. Keep repeating the affirmation and observe how the responses on the right-side change. A powerful affirmation will bring up all the negative thoughts and feelings stored deep in your consciousness and you will have the opportunity to discover what is standing between you and your goal. *The repetitive use of the affirmation will simultaneously make its impression on your mind and erase the old thought pattern, producing permanent, desirable changes in your life!*

The truth is that thoughts produce results; and since realizations can very soon be discovered with this approach, the results are often startling.

Going back to the examples of negative thoughts in the last chapter, we can use the technique just explained to change a negative to a positive in the subconscious mind. Take the belief that, "Men hurt me." As Abraham/ Hicks says, "A belief is just a thought you keep thinking." You can change your belief by thinking a different thought. To turn this around, you could say, "Men always want what is best for me," and see what negative beliefs still come up. Then the exercise would go like this:

Men always want what is best for me.

Like hell they do!

Men always want what is best for me.

No way.

Men always want what is best for me

No. I feel like crying.

Men always want what is best for me.

Why should they?

Men always want what is best for me.

Dad ignored me.

Men always want what is best for me.

I don't deserve the best.

Men always want what is best for me.

I'm not that great.

Men always want what is best for me.

Like hell they do!

Men always want what is best for me.

How could they?

Men always want what is best for me.

Can't imagine it.

Men always want what is best for me.

Tell me about it!
Men always want what is best for me.
You can't trust men.
Men always want what is best for me.
Could you trust a man? Could men care about me?
Men always want what is best for me.
Maybe they do.
Men always want what is best for me.
Can it be true?

Don't stop writing the affirmations and your reactions until no more negative responses come up. When you can write the affirmation, and feel neutral, then your subconscious mind is being programmed with no interference.

As another example, remember the male who carried the negative thought that, "Women want to suffocate (kill) me." This could be turned around to say, "Women always give me health and strength." Writing it over and over might produce responses like this:

Women always give me health and strength.
That's a laugh.
Women always give me health and strength.
They give me nothing but trouble.
Women always give me health and strength.

This is making me sad.

Women always give me health and strength.

Mother nags me.

Women always give me health and strength.

They don't even notice me.

Women always give me health and strength.

I can't trust them.

Women always give me health and strength.

Wish I could believe it.

Women always give me health and strength.

My throat aches; I want to cry.

Women always give me health and strength.

They won't even let me cry.

Women always give me health and strength.

I am afraid.

Women always give me health and strength.

Feeling confusion.

Women always give me health and strength.

Seems very risky.

Women always give me health and strength.

Might be possible.

Women always give me health and strength.

Wouldn't count on it.

Women always give me health and strength.

Maybe.

Women always give me health and strength.

Why shouldn't they?

These affirmation exercises will make you aware of what is already in your subconscious and will tell you how to make it work for you immediately. All you need is a willingness to look at yourself and a pen and paper or a computer—whatever is most comfortable for you.

After about a week of writing an affirmation, or when you have gotten in touch with most of the negative responses your mind makes to the affirmation, it is a good idea to stop using the response column and just keep writing the positive, affirming sentence. At this point you might want to switch to a recording device on your smart phone. I have found that it is just as effective for me to type affirmations; I am able to get ten written for each one I can do in longhand. Do what feels best for you.

Here is how to get the most out of the affirmations you do:

1. Work with one or more every day. The best times are just before sleeping, before starting the day, or when you are feeling troubled.

2. Write each affirmation ten or twenty times.

3. Include your name in the affirmation. Say and write each affirmation to yourself in the first, second, and third person as follows:

    a.   I, Sondra, forgive my mother for hurting me.

b. *You, Sondra, forgive your mother for hurting you.*

c. *She, Sondra, forgives her mother for hurting her.*

Writing in the second and third person is often important, since your conditioning from others came to you in this manner.

4. Continue working with the affirmations daily until they become totally integrated into your consciousness. You will know this when your mind responds positively, and when you begin to experience the intended results. You will then experience mastery over your goals. You will be using your mind to serve you.

5. Record your affirmations on cassette tapes and play them back when you can. I very often play them while driving on the freeway or when I go to bed. If I fall asleep while the earphone is still in my ear and the tape is going, the autosuggestion is still working as I sleep. (I am sure you are aware that I use affirmations in all areas of my life, for problems at work, problems with health, any problems at all. You can do the same.)

6. It is effective to look into the mirror and say the affirmations to yourself out loud. Keep saying them until you are able to see yourself with a relaxed,

happy expression. Keep saying them until you eliminate all facial tension and grimaces.

7. Another method is to sit across from a partner, each of you in a straight back chair with your hands on your thighs and knees barely touching. Say the affirmation to your partner until you are comfortable doing it. Your partner can observe your body language carefully: if you squirm, fidget, or are unclear, you do not pass. He should not allow you to go on to another one until you say it very clearly without contrary body reactions and upsets. When he does pass you, go on to the next affirmation. He can say them back to you, using the second person and your name. He should continue to say them to you until you can receive them well without embarrassment. This is harder than it sounds.

Another alternative at any time, of course, is to say them to yourself. You may not always feel like writing. However, writing is more powerful because more of the senses are involved.

So, as you begin reading now, note which affirmations have the greatest emotional reaction or "charge" for you and mark them as you go. Try to have a good time discovering the secrets to your own consciousness. If you ever get to a point where you begin to feel upset, shaky, or afraid about something negative you learn about yourself, don't panic. Keep writing the applicable affirmation over and over until your mind takes on the new thought. As it does, the negativity will be erased and you will feel lighter and better. Remember: It is just as easy to think positively as negatively. In fact, it is easier. Negative thinking takes more effort.

Don't settle for so little in your life! You deserve a lot!

Beginning Affirmation Exercises:

1. I, _____, was born with a limitless capacity for loving and fulfilling relationships.
2. I, _____, have a basic trust that my affirmations always work and my efforts will be rewarded.
3. I, _____, am willing to move through my barriers of ignorance, fear, and anger, so that my perfect being can express itself in all my relationships.
4. Loving relationships are a key element in my state of general health and well-being.
5. Every negative thought automatically triggers my creative mind to think of three desirable positive thoughts.

Markus says this about affirmations:
There is a subtle part in this process of affirmations that

requires us to step out of "thinking" that says, "How can I ever get over these negative thoughts?" In **A Course in Miracles** there is a Lesson, "I am as God created me." (Lesson #94 in the Workbook). We need to ask ourselves, "Did God create me 'not good enough', or 'out of balance', or "inadequate'?" Whatever your negative thoughts are about yourself and life, you made them up, and these are attracting negative experiences to you, even though these thoughts are not really true. You may "think" they are true because your experience confirms them, but these thoughts preceded your experience.

To stop attracting unwanted results we first have to see how we think. To think such as, "My 'good' is accompanied also by my 'bad'," produces opposing results. We project a dualistic world (of opposites) in our life because thought itself is dualistic. This is why the great sages suggest we come to a neutral place in the mind that is still and empty, a place in the mind in which we are not projecting opposites. Then we can make contact with a unified Mind, one that is connected to Divine Forces that extend only the Truth to us. Love, Peace, Joy, Happiness, Forgiveness, and Gratitude are the attitudes/thoughts of a Mind that is aligned with its true Divine Connection. And if you do not feel these in all levels of your being, including your body and emotions, then you have something to clear.

When we are working with affirmations, the negative

thoughts that are their "opposites" are false thoughts. Therefore, they only exist to the degree we are attached to thinking they are true. We have to shift this way of thinking. We have to be certain that memories and thoughts are either aligned with the Truth, "I am as God created me," or they are not. If they are not, then they can easily be let go because they do not exist in Absolute reality. Even their negative experiences are "past", and therefore not around now, so therefore over and gone. This is the true meaning of forgiveness—thoughts that are not True as God created them have no real consequences, therefore they can be let go. Why not affirm the Truth and let the rest go? This is the effective way of working with affirmations.

A Course in Miracles is a mind training quite unlike any other. The thoughts in the Workbook for Students reprogram the mind with the Truth, and push out the false in your mind. Every lesson is an affirmation. "God's peace and joy are mine." is Lesson #105. "My present happiness is all I see." is Lesson #290. These are thoughts, affirmations of the Absolute Truth that you can adopt as your own. Why not? What do you have to lose by thinking this way? It is a stretch for the mind you have been used to, but why not give yourself affirmations and miracles of the present instead of the old status quo of your past thoughts?"

Yes. Why not? Using affirmations will change your mind more than any other thought process you can do. Try it.

Coupled with a willingness to implement these new thoughts with concrete actions in your life, you will be surprised at your new results.

6. LOVING YOURSELF

ALWAYS

I once knew a very beautiful woman who had everything, it seemed. But she was always messing up her life and she once lost everything, including most of her wealth. She was a twin and she had been born first and healthy. Her sister who had come out second had always been sick and unsuccessful in life. My client hated herself because she thought she ruined her sister's life by coming out first. She ended up thinking, "I am a bad person." So, even though she was ravishingly beautiful, men stayed away from her because she did not like herself; and she did not treat herself well at all because she thought she should punish herself.

Another woman hated herself because she could not be the baby that had died before she was born. She felt her parents wanted *that* baby instead, and they had her to "make up for the loss." She felt she could never be the one they wanted, and she hated herself. She, too, was a beautiful woman; but it did not matter because she always attracted men who beat her up in one form or another. She felt guilty that she could not be the child her parents wanted—and she made sure to punish herself. This case made me aware of a metaphysical law—guilt always demands punishment.

I have had many clients who hated themselves because they did not come out as the sex their parents wanted. And the list goes on and on. People hate themselves for a million different things. People who hate themselves often get fat and then they hate themselves more. Or they conjure up some other way to prove how bad they are. It is very hard for them to get out of self-hate unless they are aware of the strong negative thoughts they may have formed about themselves way back at birth or even in the womb.

Self-hate makes one ugly. Every person I have seen who gave up their self-hate and who forgave everything became more and more beautiful right before my eyes. This leads to another metaphysical law:

"People treat you the way you treat yourself."

Jesus said, "Love thy neighbor as *thyself.*" You cannot really define love; but once I heard this: "Love is an all existing substance noticed mostly in the absence of negative thought."

Loving yourself is ultimately having self-approval. If you love yourself, you will automatically give others the opportunity to love you. If you hate yourself, you will not allow others to love you. If your self-esteem is low and someone loves and accepts you, you will reject them, try to change them, or think they are lying.

When you blame the world for lacking love, you are creating still more negative mental mass, which makes things worse for you. Some people taking the Loving Relationships Training feel real love for the first time because they become stripped of the negativity that kept them from noticing the love in the first place. Some of this negativity is buried, and you may not know you have it. Often it takes the energy of a large group to push it out of you.

Sometimes people tell me, "My life doesn't work because I don't have the right mate." That philosophy will never work. You must *become* the right person rather than looking for the right person. In order to attract the cream of the crop, you must become the cream of the crop. To become like the person you would want for a mate, we have devised processes in the training to raise your self-esteem.

Instead of beating yourself up, if you make a mistake, try this Affirmation: "Even though I made a mistake, I still completely love and accept myself." Remember this one your whole life.

Here are some other ways to increase your self-love:

1. Acknowledge and praise yourself verbally to yourself.
2. Approve of all your own actions; learn from them.
3. Have confidence in your ability.
4. Give yourself pleasure without guilt.
5. Love your body and admire your beauty.
6. Give yourself what you want; feel that you deserve it.
7. Let yourself win—in life and in relationships.
8. Allow others in to love you.
9. Follow your own intuition.
10. See your own perfection.
11. Let yourself be rich; give up poverty.
12. Reward yourself; never punish yourself.
13. Trust yourself.
14. Nourish yourself.
15. Let yourself enjoy sex and affection.
16. Turn all your negative thoughts about yourself into affirmations.

P.S. High self-esteem is not being egotistical; "Egotism is trying to prove you're OK after you've fallen into hating yourself."

7. LOVING AND HEALING

YOUR BODY

Learning self-healing and loving your body is an important factor in your relationships. If you feel good, you can enjoy your relationship. It is amazing to see how much pain and illness people tolerate. If you understand that all pain is the effort involved in clinging to a negative thought, then you can locate the negative thoughts that cause the pain and you can change those thoughts. All symptoms, therefore, are also caused by clinging to a negative thought. If you keep clinging to that thought, you could create an actual disease. This can ruin a relationship. I support a couple in learning how to heal themselves of all conditions in the body. Spiritual healing consists of these points.

- ❖ *You have to find the cause of the condition.*
- ❖ *You confess to a higher power you have been addicted to the negative thoughts causing this condition.*
- ❖ *You change the negative thoughts to positive ones.*
- ❖ *You do spiritual practices to release these thoughts.*

You can easily find out the cause of your symptoms. The cause will always be due to a negative thought. So, you need to do a simple truth process like this:

1. The negative thoughts I had that caused this condition were _____.
    (You write them out, 1, 2, 3, etc.)
2. My payoffs for keeping this condition are _____. (A "payoff" is some neurotic benefit you are getting out of this.)
3. My fears of giving up this condition are _____. (You write them out. You must have a fear, or you would not still have the condition.)
4. The affirmations I now need to think are _____. (Write down the opposite of all those negative thoughts.)

I have also learned in Liberation Breathing that people often start hating their bodies at birth. I have had clients who made the decision, "My body causes me pain," as they were being born and experiencing trauma. Then, because they had that thought, they created bodies that were filled with pain for most of their lives. (Whatever you believe to be true, you create.) Eventually it became "too much" and they even wanted to die in order to be free. And since much of the pain from the birth trauma is stored in the body, and, in some cases, is felt constantly, it is no wonder that our ancestors left their bodies. It was too painful to stay in them after years of accumulating negative mental mass.

It *is* hard to love your body when it hurts. That is, of course, when you need to love it the most because it is trying to teach you something.

After my father died, I had a pain in my body that migrated to different places. I had this pain for thirteen years, and I tried to heal it with psychiatrists, regular physicians, physical therapists, and hypnotists, with a few "medicine men" thrown in. Nothing worked. It wasn't until I did breathwork and breathed out my pain and my death urge permanently that it went away. It went away totally after three sessions! So now you can see why I became a Breathworker.

Now that I am living in a body free of tension and pain, my body is a pleasurable place to be. It makes me want to live because I always feel good. It makes me want to extend life. It makes me easier to be around. By the way, just sleeping next to someone who has cleared out the bulk of the birth trauma and death urge is a whole and new wonderful experience. There is, in fact, a new vibration to your cells (they "sing") once you clear out that negative mental mass. If you don't love your body, you don't love yourself. And if you don't love yourself, how can you expect someone else to love you or your body? Your body is your perfect mirror of yourself. It is like a computer print-out. You can clear your body as you clear your mind. It is never too late.

How often has your physical pain or illness made you grumpy and hard to live with? How often have your physical ailments affected your relationships? Conversely, how often have the ailments been the result of a relationship that you are not handling? I know of a woman who keeps getting sick because she is in the wrong relationship. So my point is sometimes the relationship itself makes you sick!

8. GIVING UP ANGER

Many of my clients grew up in families where constant fights were raging. Often these families loved each other underneath it all, but they had no idea how to express love. They did know how to handle anger. The children of these families ended up with the idea that love *was* anger. In other words, they did not feel they were being loved unless they were being yelled at! They actually had it wired up so that anger was love. In their relationships, they would create situations to make their partners really angry so they would be yelled at. They actually liked being yelled at; however, nothing ever got resolved. My work with them, Liberation Breathing and the LRT, helped them to unwire anger and love.

A Course in Miracles says that, "Anger is never justified." (ACIM, CH 30; VI; 1) It involves blame and victimhood. It states that, "You will attack [get angry at] what does not satisfy, and thus you will not see you made it up." (ACIM; CH 30; IV; 1) That means you will get angry at someone and blame them instead of looking at your thoughts which attracted what was not wanted.

This is a common pattern. Then people say, "But so and so ripped me off, so I have a right to be angry." *A Course in Miracles* says this about that: "Beware of the temptation to perceive yourself unfairly treated." In other words, it is very tempting to blame the other. But why did you create that person doing it to you?

So, after studying *ACIM* for many years I became clear that I needed to help people give up anger totally rather than encourage them to express it. Many teachers however teach how to "fight fair" since they think fighting is "normal." People often defend anger. Once a highly-trained therapist gave me a long lecture defending anger. I let him express his beliefs and I prayed that he would understand after we studied *ACIM*. I had each student teach a lesson to the class. By a miracle, he got a lesson that focused precisely on anger. After he read it he stood up and confessed, "All my life I have defended anger. Now after reading this lesson, I see that I was wrong." I even came across a guide whose author asserts that those who don't fight simply don't care about life! There are other, more sane ways for handling upsets. I will share them in a minute.

As a former nurse, I have to remind you that anger is very dangerous to your body. It raises your blood pressure, lowers your immune system, screws up your digestion and will eventually lead to disease. Ammachi says that anger makes you weak in every cell of your body!

As far as how it affects your relationships, here is what ACIM would say:

"Anger provokes separation." So, there you have it—you push people away from you with your anger. Spiritually the consequences are even worse. Hostility shuts out the mind of God. It is a very low frequency and makes you descend the ladder of holiness.

The Dalai Lama says this: "We lose control of our mind through hatred and anger. If our minds are dominated by anger, we will lose the best part of human intelligence—wisdom. Anger is one of the most serious problems facing the world today."

What do you do about it then?

My guru Babaji says this:

❖ *Don't stuff your anger. That hurts you.*
❖ *Don't dump your anger on someone else. That hurts them.*

❖ *Instead, find the thought that causes your anger, change it, and breathe out the bad energy. I have never heard a higher teaching.*

To be realistic, there will be times when you get upset about things. What to do? My husband and I handle it this way:

❖ I might say, "I am feeling activated." (So, then I am acknowledging I am upset and I am not stuffing it. I am not dumping on him either.)

❖ Then I would say: "The negative thought I am having that makes me feel activated is this _____."

❖ I express the thought without yelling or raising my voice. I chose to change it. If I feel charged still, I can take a cold shower, run around the block a few times, or even better—get a Liberation Breathing session.

The Course in Miracles Explanation by Kenneth Wapnick (a booklet published by the Foundation for Inner Peace) says this:

"Hate and anger are but attempts to project guilt from within ourselves onto another person. Anger, according to the Course, always involves such projection, no matter how justified it appears to be. The external situation is never a sufficient explanation for our hostile reactions."

Only the ego values anger. The more we attack, the guiltier we become, and the greater our need to project and attack again. Remember that *blame is always off the track*. Whenever you feel like blaming your mate or another, *Stop!* Take a look to see what the response that makes you feel like blaming says about you and how you might have created that response.

The problem is that the ego is addicted to anger. *ACIM* says the first obstacle to peace is the desire to get rid of peace! So, if you are addicted to anger you have to do spiritual practices to clear the habit. If you have anger, it means you have not forgiven people. You need to forgive everyone 100% and that will dissolve your anger. People often tell me, "But I can't forgive so and so." It is not that they can't. It is that they *won't*. It is a stubborn refusal. Forgiveness is a decision. Forgiveness is the key to happiness.

Remember this: You cannot be enlightened and keep your anger.

What is your forgiveness level on your mother? 0-10 (10 is total complete forgiveness. Zero is none) what number do you get? You can check yourself:

❖ What is your forgiveness level on your father? (Pick a number.)

45

❖ What is your forgiveness level on your mother?

❖ What is your forgiveness level on your siblings?

❖ What is your forgiveness level on ex-spouses?

❖ What is your level of forgiveness on any step-parent?

❖ What is your forgiveness level on yourself?

If you are not at ten on these, you are still angry. The problem is this: What you don't forgive, you attract. So you will get a mate who has that same fault until you forgive it. Also, when you don't forgive someone, you are tied to them by "aka cords" (psychic attachments,) so this makes you become more like the person you hate.

Jesus said you should forgive 70 times 7. I finally found out why. In numerology that represents completion—490. So I made up the *Forgiveness Diet* in my book *The Only Diet There Is*. In this book, I explain a simple process: for example, you write, "I forgive my mother completely," 70 times a day for 7 days. The next week you do the exercise for your father. The following week select another person. Maybe even do it on yourself if your forgiveness level is low.

If it does not work, and you are still feeling very "charged," even after you have done the *Forgiveness Diet* for seven days on a person, then you are really stubborn. Getting a number 9 on forgiveness level is not good enough. *ACIM* says if you have not forgiven 100% you have not forgiven at all. To handle stubbornness, try writing the

THE NEW LOVING RELATIONSHIPS BOOK

following prayer 108 times in one sitting: "I pray to God, a power greater than myself, for the willingness to change."

In closing this chapter, I quote two female gurus. I have met both of them and I can assure you, they are both free of all anger. This enables them to impart intense peace to all those around them.

Guru Mai

"It is said that if you are a true ascetic, you are completely devoid of anger. If there is any trace of anger in you, you are called a scoundrel, not an ascetic. A great being will go to any extent to remove the fire of anger. The greatness of a sadhu monk is that he can drop something once he realizes he has it."

Mata Amritanandamayi—The "Mother" from the book *Awaken Children*

"Anger and impatience will always cause problems. Suppose you have a weakness for easily getting angry. Once you become normal again, go and sit in the family shrine room or in solitude and regret and repent of your own anger and sincerely pray to your beloved deity seeking help to get rid of it. Try to make your mind aware of the bad outcome of anger. When you are angry at someone, you lose your mental balance. Your power to discriminate stops functioning. You weigh whatever comes into your mind and act accordingly. You may even utter crude words. By acting and thinking with anger you lose a lot of good energy.

Become aware that these negative feelings will only pave the way for your own destruction. "

9. THE DECISION FOR PEACE

My husband, Markus, studied *A Course in Miracles* for 17 years with Tara Singh, his master. Obviously, this significant book has transformed many lives, and its focus is to help us allow a deep and lasting inner peace. Markus's contribution to our relationship has been enhanced by his serious study of the *Course*, and by his tutelage with Tara Singh, whom Dr. Schucman, the scribe of *ACIM* groomed to present workshops and retreats around the USA. This chapter is about making a real decision for peace, written by Markus.

Tara Singh, my teacher, impressed upon us the importance making a real decision. He would point out how unwilling we are to give up our thoughts, our opinions, and our conditioning. There are many choices we make in our life—what car to buy; what college to attend; what mate to choose to spend our life with; what career we pursue. These are all a few of the plethora of choices we make on a daily basis, and on a long-term basis in our life. But these choices are not at the same importance of making a decision.

Choices are about likes and dislikes, motives and intentions; a decision is something you make with God. The real decision is a willingness you apply to your whole life. What is the well-being and happiness we seek to create and have? Why are the things we seek too often so unsatisfying after a while?

We need to decide for peace; we need to decide for harmonious relationships; we need to decide to find and maintain the relationships and endeavors in life that make us feel good. Our learning at this physical plane is for the purpose of this one decision to remain in the essence of our being. Peace and Joy may be our natural state, but we have made ourselves absent from our higher self and aspirations. A decision is something of certainty. It is made with God, and it is absolute. It restores you to your most joyful being of who you really are. It is something that you make once, and never turn back, and never stop short of realizing.

There is a lesson in A Course in Miracles that states it very simply about a decision:

"Heaven is the decision I must make." Lesson #138

Who would have thought they were actually in charge of whether or not they would reach and enter Heaven? Two things are very *strikingly clear about this statement: 1) Heaven is a state of being totally in my hands to enter, and 2) I am the one who decides whether I do or not, right NOW! This is taking back my sovereignty. By making this decision with my Creator, with God, to actually enter the blissful state of oneness, of wholeness, of freedom from conflict, the flow of deep ease will enter into the vibration of all that I do. It is a serious decision that we all can make.*

Some of you will say, "Oh, my life is in a mess right now. My relationship is strained, we disagree on so many things; we do not communicate well, and have lost the sense of closeness we had in the beginning of our relationship." That could be the status quo. But a decision is a way out, and it shifts your attention on what is your birthright, instead of what are the disorders of your physical conditions. Others will say, "My life is pretty good. Why do I need to think about Heaven?" Well, how good is it? Are you under stress to maintain the "good life" you have made up for yourself? Do you really have that inner peace and joy that God wants you to have?

Thoughts are very powerful catalysts for attracting like experiences, and these can be negative or positive; fearful or loving; sorrowful or joyful. How one feels in any situation is dependent upon what thoughts one focuses on. Giving attention to something makes it more specific, more manifested, more real. We must all make this kind of decision in which there are no opposite counter-choices. Heaven is Heaven. It is the absence of "hell." In fact, the decision for Heaven is the escape from hell. You may say, "OK, how do I make such a decision?" Again, because you make it with God, God provides the "how." You need not concern yourself with that part so much; you just need to be determined to not indulge in negative thoughts and feelings.

My teacher Tara Singh said, "Heaven is always present, but you choose to be absent." That is to say we are sleeping in a kind of "nightmare" that is not our real domain. Heaven is just waiting for us to wake up into this state of our natural being. The decision for peace is similar. When Sondra and I first got back together in 2008, after nearly a twenty-year absence, we made a decision to have a "conflict-free" relationship. This is the same as deciding for Heaven when you think about it. Is there any conflict in Heaven? Obviously, by definition there is not. Peace is made by a decision. Two people agree that their meaningless thoughts, which produce doubt, conflict, suffering and upset, are just those—meaningless. They decide for peace. They decide for Heaven. Right now. Heaven and peace are not things to achieve; they are realities to be immersed in. This decision will carry you through any challenges; and help you allow solutions and miracles for yourself.

You can decide for peace. What is keeping you from doing this in your relationship? Do you want to be right? Do you want to feel dominated and suppressed? Do you want to be in control? Do you want to be continually discontented? Another lesson in ACIM states:

"I want the peace of God." Lesson # 185

Do you? You say you do. But do you really? Would there be any conflict in your relationship if you wanted peace above all else? Try it. What do you have to lose? Make the decision for Heaven, and only that. Only peace will satisfy you. All else in your relationship that is not supreme joy, perfect happiness, is just a bad dream. You can wake up.

10. CLEARING UP THE

FOURTEEN PATTERNS

A man named Herb once told me that after his divorce he had dated many women and he had noticed that they were all like his ex-wife. He said they could have all been right out of the same mold. They were all destructive to his life and yet he could not stop himself from attracting this type of woman. He felt he might as well have been addicted to booze or drugs; he recognized this syndrome as being like an addiction. He was, however, smart enough not to marry any of these women or he probably would have been divorced over and over again.

After he learned about the fourteen patterns in the LRT, he was amazed at how simple it all was. Each woman was like the stepfather he hated. Once he was able to forgive his stepfather, he stopped attracting that kind of woman.

A woman in one training session jumped up and started screaming, "My God, I have been marrying my nanny." She had been raised by a bitchy, English nanny—and all the men she married were like her. She was on her fourth husband!

Once you get out of these "patterns," life is totally different. Until then, there is a tendency to go through an endless stream of parental substitutes for mates.

Have you ever found yourself doing the same thing in every new relationship, even though you hoped things would be different when you got a "new" partner? If so, you are probably stuck in a "pattern." A pattern is a repetitive unconscious behavior. This is descriptive of the tendencies I have seen in relationships—at least in the old neurotic relationships of the past. Clearing out these patterns is imperative to having good relationships. Here are fourteen patterns I have identified that continue to show up in relationships. I'm sure there are more; however, these seem to be the most common.

Pattern #1

There is a tendency to create a partner who is the same personality type as one of your parents.

Pattern #2

There is a tendency to create a partner who treats you the same way your parents treated you.

Pattern #3

There is a tendency to copy the kind of relationship your parents had with each other.

Pattern#4

There is a tendency to attract and receive disapproval from your mate if your parents disapproved of you a lot.

Pattern #5

There is a tendency to set up a win-lose relationship due to unresolved sibling rivalry.

Pattern #6

There is a tendency to get even and get revenge on parents by taking your hostility at them out on your mate — i.e., projection of anger onto your mate.

Pattern #7

There is a tendency to want to remain a helpless child waiting for your mate to take care of you. We call this in the LRT the "will you take care of me syndrome." You would be surprised how much it runs the dynamics of a relationship.

Pattern #8

There is a tendency to create struggle in relationships because one is addicted to struggle at birth. Having an easy, smooth relationship is too threatening and too unfamiliar.

Pattern #9

There is a tendency to use family members as scapegoats wherein you take out your frustration and stress on them.

Pattern #10

There is a tendency to use control and domination if you have a need to be "right." This creates darkness is a relationship.

Pattern #11

There is a tendency to channel the mind of the blood family. You might be channeling your mother's mind, your father's mind or the whole family mind.

Pattern#12

There is a tendency to set up incestuous triangles because of unresolved sexual energy in the family.

Pattern #13

There is a tendency to punish oneself or get punished because of unresolved guilt.

Pattern #14

There is a tendency to sabotage bliss and happiness because you are not used to maintaining it or you don't think you deserve it.

These patterns are elaborated on in our new book *Spiritual Intimacy*. The first step of clearing up any one of these patterns is to become conscious of it. Then you have to decide to "choose out" of it, and this includes forgiving any family members who acted it out for you. You can write affirmations that address each pattern. And then you probably would benefit from having a Liberation Breathing / Rebirthing session or attending a Loving Relationships Training.

11. MASTERING THE FIVE BIGGIES

This is probably one of the most important chapters in the book. Read it very carefully and think about the ideas a long time. Before I became aware of this information, my life did not work very well. After I became aware of this information and started handling it, my life started working really well. Need I say more? I am sure every breathworker would agree and I am sure everyone else who has cleared up these points in themselves would agree. So please, for your own sake, do not take this chapter lightly. Think about it. Take action on it. You will be *so* relieved if you do.

The "Five Biggies" are negative consciousness factors that affect most people and keep them from experiencing bliss. They were brilliantly conceived by Leonard Orr; I have adapted them specifically to relationships for the training. The five biggies are:

1. The birth trauma
2. The parental disapproval syndrome
3. Specific negatives
4. The unconscious death urge
5. Other lifetimes

We have talked about the way your birth extensively affects your relationships in other parts of this book. See the last chapter called "Liberation Breathing Explained."

The *parental disapproval syndrome* is about how parents invalidate their children the way they themselves were invalidated. These invalidations break the spirit of the child and the child loses self-esteem and sells out his or her power. We grow up so used to disapproval that we unconsciously set up our partners to give us more of the same. This syndrome alone wipes us out, and we are always feeling hurt by the disapproval we create. Our mates become our disapproving parents, and we end up eventually having to divorce our "parents" by divorcing our partners.

In the Loving Relationships Training, we take a great deal of time to clear the parental disapproval syndrome from people's consciousness. On the first day, we dissolve it as much as possible so that the next day there is space in which to create a new kind of relationship, a new kind of love.

Specific negatives are negative thought structures about yourself and about life that you carry around. These are affecting your relationships constantly. If you have a negative thought from birth such as "Life is dangerous," for example, it is easy to see how that has affected results all your life. We have already seen how affirmations clear up negatives.

It is very important to understand how the *unconscious death urge* affects your relationships. Most people have the thought that there is a source outside themselves that is going to kill them. Some day you have to get enlightened enough to take responsibility for facing the truth that *all death is suicide.* If you completely accept the law that the thinker creates with his thoughts, then you know you can change the thought that death is inevitable: "I can keep my body as long as I want and I can also tell my cells to *youth* instead of age."

Other lifetimes sometimes exert a strongly negative influence on our current life. We call this a "bleed through" when you are dragging a past life into this life. I recommend these books: *We Were Born Again to Be Together* by Dick Sutphen, and *Other Lives, Other Selves* by Dr. Roger Woolger.

12. CLEANING UP OLD

RELATIONSHIPS

The main past relationship to clear is the one with your parents because: *Anything unresolved with your parents will come up in your relationships.* Generally, the things our partners do that upset us are things we have not forgiven our parents for doing. When you have totally forgiven your parents for whatever is unresolved, either your partner will stop doing the upsetting thing or you will find another partner without that problem. It is likely that, without knowing it, your partner was trying to heal you by acting out your parents' behavior for you.

Love takes upon itself your negatives so you can see them more clearly. This means that your mate makes an unconscious attempt to heal you by acting out roles and negatives of your past so that you can process that aspect out of your consciousness. Most of us don't know that is happening, so we begin to blame our mates. Children will act out your subconscious mind so the best thing is to treat your children like they are your guru.

Eventually we must clean up all past relationships that are not completely resolved. How can you know if the relationship is cleaned up? Consider your past and present relatives, friends, and lovers. If you have any feelings for them other than unconditional love when you think of their name, then those relationships are not cleaned up. Lately I have seen clients who want a new relationship but they are unable to create that new relationship because they are still "hanging on" to a former relationship. This means there is no room for the new person to come in. They are afraid to let go of the last one because they might be alone. But they are alone because they never let go of the past one! You have to go into the void and create the space for the new person to come in.

13. STAYING CLEAR

The main thing you need to know is that Love brings up anything unlike itself. This means when your partner loves you a lot, he or she is sending you a lot of energy and this energy is so powerful that it pushes up junk from your subconscious. Your love is doing the same thing for them. So then, your mate will push up all your patterns, your suppressed anger, your guilt, your fear, etc. And you will push all that up in them. When all this starts coming up, most people argue. What we do in our community instead is to get Liberation Breathing sessions and or do processes.

You have a big responsibility to maintain clarity. A humble person is someone who recognizes his errors, admits them and does something about them. When you are with someone like that, you are very, very fortunate.

I often see couples where one is willing to practice self-analysis and the other is not. This combination rarely works. The partner willing to process usually grows a lot faster than the other and it becomes obvious that they do not have similar levels of commitment to the path of enlightenment. If you find yourself in this situation, you need to look at why you created this situation for yourself and to decide if it is right for you to stay.

Ask yourself: What is my payoff for being with someone who is not willing to clear?

How does this situation mirror my past?

Am I using this person to hold me back?

The spiritual master Yogananda teaches that self-analysis is the key to the mastery of life. He has also stated that, without self-analysis, man leads a robot-like life.

"People who never analyze themselves are like mechanical products in the factory of their environment. They are preoccupied with breakfast, lunch and dinner, working and sleeping and being entertained. They don't know what or why they are seeking, nor why they never realize complete happiness." —Yogananda

The Bible says, "Be ye perfect even as God is perfect." That is an assignment. The only way to have a perfect relationship is if both people are willing to experience their own perfection. To experience your own perfection, you must release the ego's thought system. And in a relationship, you both have to be committed to this. If there is resistance to self-analysis, find out why. Of course, that too requires self-analysis.

Self-analysis can be as simple as this:

- ❖ The negative thoughts I had which created this situation were_____.
- ❖ The desired outcome of this situation is_____.
- ❖ The new thoughts or affirmations I need to think about to achieve this desired outcome are_____.

Until we are all spiritual masters, we will always have something to clear. There is always something higher, so one might as well get used to clearing. If both you and your partner are on the path of enlightenment and equally involved in Spiritual Purification to clear yourselves, processing can be enjoyable. Helping each other stay clear can be a fun game! If your mate is miserable, you can help them find the negative thought that is making them miserable. Never process someone without their permission, however.

If Markus or I get stuck, we simply request a breathing session dry or wet. It is a beautiful intimate thing if he wants

THE NEW LOVING RELATIONSHIPS BOOK

to get in the bathtub with the snorkel and do Liberation Breathing to clear himself while asking me to be present to support him. This is one way we avoid arguments.

67

14. CLEANING UP YOUR RELATIONSHIP DAILY

I remember one couple (and many others) that had the following pattern: Dave would be angry with Janet for something, but he would not tell her. He would decide maybe he shouldn't tell her and then he would pretend to "get over it." But he would be seething inside. Janet had the exact same tendency. She would never tell Dave what made her angry with him. They would both "stuff it." Then the pressure would build and build and finally they would have a knock-down drag-out fight and scream out all the things they had stored up. This was "dumping" on the highest order. They were always fighting about things that happened two months ago, sometimes even a year ago. They were never in present time and one or the other would always deny that they said or did that thing two months ago. Then they would get in a fight about a fight. It was a mess.

After taking the LRT, they literally started *all over*. They confessed to me that they had both been suicidal before the training because they could not seem to get themselves out of this syndrome. They made a simple agreement afterwards to clean up their relationship every night or on the spot if possible—but at least every night. They both stuck to this agreement and it worked. Besides, they found out that they were not really upset with each other for the reasons they thought and there was not much to fight about anymore. But when something did come up, they would express it on the same day and start each new day fresh as though they had a "new" relationship.

It is a good policy to have an agreement in your present relationship that you will clean things up at least every night. It is better to clean up things on the spot, but sometimes that is not appropriate. But if you want a light, joyful relationship, don't wait another day to communicate something. My mother always said "Never let the sun set on your anger; it is in the Bible Sondra."

Each night you can simply say to your roommate, lover, or spouse, "Is there anything you need to communicate to me before we go to sleep?" If you do this, then nothing builds up and each new day starts well. Eventually this process will become integrated into your life as a good habit and you won't need to ask the questions to remind each other.

After you have had breathwork, you will hunger to communicate these things the same day; waiting any longer will be too uncomfortable in your body because you will be extra sensitive to all vibrations.

The amount of love that flows between the two of you is often controlled by the quantity and quality of your communications. After you have cleaned up the day's withheld communications, complete the process by acknowledging yourself and your partner for successes. Then you can drop off to sleep in a happy state of mind, or have sex without a lot of "psychic garbage" between you.

15. HAVING A LIFE LONG

SPIRITUAL PATH

You need a spiritual practice that you can count on to keep your relationship in tune. Personally, I cannot imagine not having Liberation Breathing in my life. I have been able to get through all kinds of traumas and dramas by breathing them out in the presence of another. For me it is Heaven to have a husband who is a breath worker like myself. We can give each other sessions instead of needing therapy. Liberation Breathing is not therapy. It is a spiritual purification technique for clearing anything. You can even clear your birth trauma!

What does your birth experience have to do with your

relationships? More than you ever dreamed! All of the following emotional responses are closely related to your birth:

- ❖ Fear of entrapment in a relationship
- ❖ Womb-like dependency on a mate
- ❖ Fear of pleasure
- ❖ Separation anxiety
- ❖ Fear of letting go with people
- ❖ Fear of receiving love; distrust of people
- ❖ Sexual problems
- ❖ Poor self-image; feeling less than another
- ❖ Feeling like you are dying when a partner leaves you
- ❖ Suppressed anger and rage and more!

Our research has shown that the roots of these common problems go back to the womb and the first five minutes of life. Before Rebirthing was discovered, it was very hard to get down to the personal lies (negative core beliefs) formed at birth that govern our lives. I like to say that this will likely be the first generation of people whose relationships really work because they are dealing with the birth-death cycle.

Liberation Breathing not only cures permanently the fears that ruin relationships, but it also heals you in every way. As you breathe out negative mental mass, retained from birth, you feel healthier, more alive, more beautiful, and more lovable. You naturally begin to attract fabulous

72

people into your life with whom it is easy to have a loving, exciting relationship.

Some examples of the decisions I made at birth that have always affected my relationships with men were these:

1. I can't love this. It hurts. Life hurts.
2. I can't trust men if this is what they are going to do to me.
3. Men can't be depended upon when I need them.
4. This is too much. I hate you. Stay out of my life.

With thoughts like these it is a wonder I allowed any man to get close to me. The truth is that at the beginning of a relationship thoughts like this tend to be suppressed. But once love begins to flow, the thoughts start to surface. (This is because love brings up anything unlike itself.) Those subconscious thoughts would begin to rear their ugly heads and produce results, even though I was no longer consciously thinking them. When enough thoughts came up, the relationship would blast apart. (This usually happens when both partners' patterns are surfacing at the same time.)

Since I had buried thoughts from birth like "Men aren't there for me" and "Stay out of my life," having a man stay with me was not compatible with my programming. Therefore, I would have to create his leaving to support my pattern; it is like supporting a drug or alcohol habit. The men, even if they loved me very, very much, would run up against my pattern and find they had to give me what I expected — which was *not* to be there. So if they tried to stay, I would set them up to leave.

Before I became conscious, I did not know I had these buried thoughts. It was next to impossible to recognize the thoughts as my own, and my relationships always ended up the same. It has taken the energy of the LRT, the energy of Liberation Breathing, and the energy of God and affirmations to blast these out of me.

A *personal lie* is your most negative thought about yourself, usually formed at birth. Now you can see how important it is to become aware of your own personal lies if you want to have good relationships. Here are some examples of personal lies:

- ❖ I am not good enough
- ❖ I am bad
- ❖ I am wrong
- ❖ I am not perfect
- ❖ I am weak
- ❖ I am guilty
- ❖ I can't
- ❖ I am not capable
- ❖ I am a failure
- ❖ Something is wrong with me
- ❖ I am a disappointment
- ❖ I am not wanted.

You need to uncover your own particular "personal lie" with the help of a well-trained breathworker. I have collected over three hundred different lies, believe it or not.

Liberation Breathing is not just about working out your birth trauma.

It is to liberate you from all suffering. It is very valuable for working on relationships issues in general. For example, many people fear intimacy. This can be released. Many people are addicted to anger in relationships. This can be released. Many people are too guilty to be able to have fun in relationships. This can be released. Many people have a fear of being hurt around relationships. This can be released. Most people are stuck in negative thoughts that ruin their relationships. They can be released.

Liberation Breathing also puts you in a higher "frequency" and when you feel that, you can have a much better time in relationships.

Markus and I give sessions together and this is very valuable for any client as they have the male–female energy together. Clearing on the subject of relationships is our specialty. We can even give sessions via skype if you are interested.

16. COMMUNICATING WELL

The quality of your relationships is directly related to the quality of your communication skills. But if you grew up in a household where parents gave each other the silent treatment, OR where one parent dominated the communication, OR where there was a lot of yelling, OR where one was afraid to speak up, then you were given a model that impeded clear communication. What often happens in intimate relationships is that the couple is copying their parents' way and/or taking out anger on the mate. Then the communication starts to contain abusive behavior such as being demanding, bossy, irritable, sarcastic, putting down, being parental or condescending. Intimidation becomes a problem. Being parental becomes a problem. Being childish becomes a problem.

If the above situations are happening, ask yourself: would I be talking like this to anyone else? It would seem that the person we are in love with deserves the sweetest and most gentle communication before anyone else. But too often the opposite happens. You would never speak to a friend like that. Your mate gets to be your target. Taking *blame* out of the communication is vital.

The best form of communication is called Compassionate Communication or non-violent communication from Dr. Rosenberg. It goes like this:

A. "Something I notice in our relationship is_____."

B. "The way I feel about this is_____."

C. "What I need and recommend about this is_____."

Try to avoid *you* sentences. Remain sweet and gentle while expressing feelings.

Communication is affected by your self-image. If you have a low self-image you may be shy about expressing yourself. People with good self-esteem speak up.

Oprah stated that the main thing she learned in twenty-five years was that people want to be heard. This statement inspired me and Markus to come up with a technique for listening. We call it the eight-minute process.

1. You go to a fine restaurant with soft music and a carpet on the floor so it is quiet. (Maybe in a hotel.)
2. You sit down and the person who is the most activated begins speaking using non-violent communication.
3. The one listening must observe these rules:
    a. No interrupting
    b. No bad faces.
    c. No rehearsing what you are going to answer.
4. The communicator speaks for eight minutes while the listener listens
5. Then you switch places. The speaker is now the listener.
6. After you have *heard* each other, you have a sweet discussion. Imagine you are talking to your best friend.

This approach is very effective. Some couples experiencing stress found that they had to do this eight-minute process daily for a while. Practicing the speaking-listening process in the bath works also.

17. TELLING THE COMPLETE TRUTH FASTER

Because children are psychic and can often read people's minds, and even at times see their auras, they might blurt out something that not only seems weird to a parent, but something that is hard on the parent's nerves such as, "Mommie, I saw purple around Uncle Harry's head!" or "Uncle Bill really hates Aunt Sarah and he wishes she'd die." About this time a mother might, in fact, punish the child for saying such ridiculous things. After that a child might decide that if he tells the truth, he will be punished. Then, he tends to grow up either telling lies in order to save his ass or to avoid telling what he sees and feels. Probably, he will "lose" or suppress his ability to see auras and distinguish the truth.

I have found that it is very hard to keep a relationship clean when the truth is suppressed. I have found that it is very hard to clean up a relationship when people are afraid to tell the truth.

One has to begin by using affirmations like these:

"It is now safe for me to tell the truth."
"I can tell my true feelings safely."
"People love it when I tell the truth."
"Telling the truth always heals."

Werner Erhard of Erhard Seminars Training or *EST* once said, "What you can't communicate runs you." I certainly agree. People are telepathic, whether you like it or not, so don't try to fool anybody for a second. The body never lies. Some people say that communication is 40 percent verbal and 60 percent nonverbal. This means that you are easy to read if you are suppressing something. Suppression is also painful and harmful to your body.

People are afraid to tell each other some things because they think they might hurt the other person or themselves. Well, it hurts you both much more if you fail to communicate whatever it is. First of all, your body will be in pain if you are withholding communication; second, the other person will become confused; and third, the relationship will get crazy. The truth will come out eventually anyway, and by then the mistrust and anger may be so great that the whole relationship will blow up.

The Truth works. The truth heals.

Tell it as fast as you can. Tell what the truth is for you right now. People will love you for it. You will feel good for doing it. Tell how you *feel!* Of course, you need to be tactful. If you are sweet with your words and if you are not into blame or criticism, it is refreshing. Withholding words builds resentment. What I cannot stand is the feeling I must be really careful what I say and I feel like I am walking on eggs. Notice how you can say anything to your best friend and it works. It works because you say it respectfully. Your mate should be like your best friend.

18. FINDING THE HIGHEST

SPIRITUAL THOUGHT

Many couples I have worked with argue because they each get stuck on their "position." He thinks for sure he is right, and she thinks for sure she is right. Neither will budge from their position and they continue to fight. This could go on for years. I assure you, there *is* another way to play the game and it is also exciting.

Marvin and Thelma were fighting about whether or not they should move. Thelma said they had outgrown the house and there was not enough room anymore for their things. She felt crowded and depressed; and besides the house was always damp and musty because of its location. This problem had gotten worse over the years, and there seemed to be no way to get rid of the dampness. Marvin said they could never get another house for that amount of money and they could not afford anything else. They fought about this continually. They went 'round and 'round and 'round and there was never a resolution. I told them it was time to *go for solution* and that there was a higher spiritual thought. That thought was that they could *both* win. It had never occurred to them, for some reason that they could both win.

I asked them to try seeing things a new way. I asked them to entertain the thought that they *could* find a house that was spacious, dry and warm at a reasonable price. Or they could surrender to the thought that they could get rid of some things and find some way to clear up the dampness. Both thoughts were positive as opposed to the two negative positions that they had earlier. The first step was that at least they each got off their negative positions. The next step was to find the highest thought that would enable each to get what they wanted. They chose to move. Because Marvin surrendered to a higher thought than the one he had (he went from "It is impossible" to "It might be possible") they did in fact find a new house at a reasonable price. It was in fact only a little bit more, but because there were more rooms, Thelma was able to start a mail order business and they soon had more money plus a new house.

There is always another way where both of you can win.

Never allow yourself to stay stuck in any position. Always be willing to discover and accept a higher spiritual thought. You can always feel and know which is the highest thought by listening to your body. The highest thought is always the one that is most positive, the least limiting, and the most productive. It "feels" the best in your body. This game prevents power struggles and fights. People learn to play the game in the training and are always developing their skill.

Each person's being willing to surrender to the highest spiritual thought does not imply that someone gives power to another. Sometimes one may have the higher spiritual thought, and sometimes the other partner will have it. If my partner has it, I leave my position and rise to the level of the higher thought. If I have the higher thought, my partner does the same. Here is what we do to avoid fighting:

In summary:

1.   When there is a strong difference of opinion on anything — don't fight.
2.   Decide to *go for solution.*
3.   Decide to find the highest thought for the solution.
4.   Drop your "positions" and the need to be right.
5.   Start with a blank slate.
6.   Start by guessing what is the highest thought for solution. (The highest thought—either of you can come up with it—is the following:
     a.   The most positive

THE NEW LOVING RELATIONSHIPS BOOK

b. The most loving

c. The most productive

d. Feels best in your body

e. Both people like it

7. Go back and forth and channel high thoughts as possible solutions.

    You can tell when the highest thought is on the floor because it feels good.

8. If your mate channels the highest thought, you gladly go up to that thought.

9. If you channel the highest thought, your mate gladly goes up to that thought.

10. You do not argue about which is the highest thought. If you get two that are close and you cannot decide, you part and meditate and ask a higher power.

In business meetings or other group situations, you can evolve the highest thought. When the highest thought has been presented and everyone recognizes it, then people stop being "stuck" and rise to the new level. Everyone is relieved and happy no matter who came up with the thought. Teach people at work how to play this game. It really helps meetings.

Work on your own to upgrade the level of your thoughts, and ask your partner to do the same. It is a spiritual discipline to constantly raise the quality of your

thoughts moment by moment. You will be amazed at the results.

19. GIVING UP GUILT

Once my business partner and I were shocked to find ourselves in a pattern of losing things. We each had lost gold jewelry, money, and some very good clothes. We set our minds to figure this out before it got worse.

We finally realized that we were suffering from guilt because we were having it too good and we were having too much fun. (People in our culture often get the idea that pleasure is bad and even that "good is bad." You don't dare have it "too good," whatever that is.) Compared to most people, we were having too much fun and so we had to balance it out by getting rid of some things in order to not feel guilty. We then decided that we had to get rid of guilt instead of getting rid of "things." We came up with the joke of giving up guilt for Lent!

Shortly after that we left for Denver. On the way to Kennedy Airport, we got behind a funeral procession. My business partner looked at me and quipped, "It is the death of guilt." I laughed and we got on the plane. In Denver we got off the plane and lo and behold, three graduates who picked us up came in an old hearse! We took guilt to the grave and the problem cleared up.

Guilt very often "runs" or controls relationships. This includes your relationship with money! Guilt is a symptom (much in the same way that fever is a symptom) that something is out of kilter in your relationship with the universe. If you are clear that you are a perfect manifestation of the Source, then guilt makes no sense. So guilt arises when we let ourselves forget our own divinity.

Many people go along letting their relationships work well and giving themselves a lot of pleasure until they suddenly reach their pleasure tolerance. This is an artificial barrier they have set up for themselves which is controlled by guilt. The minute they start feeling guilty for having a wonderful relationship or for having an abundance of money, they will begin messing it up. You have to work out guilt in order to believe you deserve a good relationship. You have to work out guilt to allow yourself to have all the pleasure that comes along with a perfect relationship. And you have to work out guilt to handle money successfully.

There is likely to be past life guilt. There is also religious guilt. There is probably guilt for hurting one's mother at birth. Then there is more guilt about things we did that were bad or that did not turn out well. There is a lot of guilt.

A Course in Miracles (which is a correction of religion) says this:

"Guilt is not only not of God, it is an attack on God."

David Hawkins said this: "Excessive guilt and remorse are disguised forms of egotism in which the self becomes blown up, exaggerated, and the hero of the tragedy, the negativity of which feeds the ego. Wallowing in guilt is an indulgence. The error is inflated instead of being relinquished to a higher power. By spiritual alignment, he says, the past circumstances underlying the guilt are re-contextualized under the influence of spiritual energy. The question one has to face is whether one wishes to cling to it and thereby get the "juice" or give it up. This is the point of decision without which healing cannot occur. (Mistakes are intrinsic to the learning process.)

The recovery from guilt is confession, forgiveness, penance and the renewal and rededication to spiritual principles and good works, selfless service and humanitarian efforts.

Guilt always demands punishment. So how have you been punishing yourself?

20. BLESSING INSTEAD OF JUDGING

Although blessing instead of judging is an ancient practice, it might be new for you to bless those whom you want to judge. The Kahunas of Hawaii teach that even mentally criticizing others affects your body. Verbally it is worse of course. Criticism kills relationships. The Kahunas teach that criticism of the self or of others causes stress and inhibits awareness, memory and energy flow, making you weaker and more susceptible to illness. The Bible teaches us that someone who is thankful for everything will be made glorious and that attitudes of love, praise and gratitude fill one with incomprehensible power of the Spirit. We may know these ideas, but applying them at all times can be challenging. When someone displays a behavior that is intolerable, we usually don't feel like blessing them. To break the habit of judging that person, try blessing the situation instead. Support the person who is moving through the offensive pattern, bless them, see them as healed of it, and honor and respect their God Self. This is easier to do if the relationship is already placed in the context of conscious blessing.

Blessing what you want daily and focusing on praise as a habit will create a safe space in your relationship. A sense of peace and relaxation should be the context of any relationship; and this should be re-established daily—telepathically and verbally. If a couple makes a point of focusing on praise as a daily discipline, preferably in a sacred space (such as before an altar) then everything that happens is placed in that context. When that context is repeatedly re-established, each partner becomes more willing to resolve issues and work out his or her own dark shadows with the support and encouragement of the other. If your mate knows, with certainty, that you continually bless him and don't judge his true being, he won't be threatened by discussing those actions or habits that need to be corrected for him to become enlightened.

However, if someone has come from a home where criticism and verbal abuse were common, he may not only expect criticism, but he may try to draw that same behavior out of his mate. This is because the mind seeks familiarity. He may unconsciously want criticism and judgment so that he will "feel at home." Or he may want to feel the familiar resentment.

Praise and gratitude might even seem suspicious to a mind addicted to criticism. This self-induced pattern is an obstacle that must be overcome.

Let's say you find yourself in a place you don't like but from which there is no escape. You feel like complaining. Instead, try asking yourself this:

"Why have I created this situation? What can I learn from this? How can I lift the resonance here? The answer is to bless the place and the situation as your teacher and to bless it as valuable even though in may not have met your standard of quality and beauty. You may actually bring about change. You can also bless everyone and everything that represents what you want.

Praise Saturation.

Many people have no idea how great they are. Perhaps they have had a lot of parental disapproval. They may be starved for acknowledgement. Praise saturation merely means you acknowledge them verbally in every way you can think of. And you do it sincerely, finding those qualities that are really great and true in that person. Say "Something I really like about you is_____."

Verbal acknowledgement works and that is all there is to it.

21. GETTING CLEAR ON

MONEY

Once I had a client who had been married to two different millionaires. They had lost all their money when they were with her. This woman was extremely intelligent and she wondered what this was about and if she had anything to do with it. During her session I found out that her father had been very wealthy. He had bet heavily at the casinos in Monte Carlo that his pregnant wife was going to have a boy. When in fact, his wife delivered a baby girl, he was not only very disappointed, but he lost a great deal of money. When this woman was growing up, she never heard the end of this story. Her father made it very plain to her that she was the cause of him losing lots of money. He told her this so many times when she was little that she believed it and she got the thought in her head, "I cause men to lose lots of money." She, of course, attracted rich men like her father who lost money when they were with her, which proved that her father must be right and that she was in fact terrible. Of course, the men she attracted had thoughts like "Women rip me off," etc., so their patterns "dovetailed."

Money arguments are a common cause of divorce. It is all so unnecessary because it is possible to clear out the negative money karma that each person brings to a relationship. Money is very important in a relationship. More upsets, arguments, and even divorce center around money than you can imagine, though the real cause of the conflict may often be something else.

Money is like love in that the amount you have is determined by how much you are willing to receive. You will have only as much as you feel comfortable having. Therefore, don't blame others for what you don't have.

Money like food obeys your instructions. Money is energy and you control its flow. The same is true of food. In fact, if you were not breast-fed adequately when you were an infant, you may be run by the idea that, "I can't get enough" or even, "I can't get any." As an adult your subconscious interprets this as "I can't get enough love" or "I can't get enough money."

THE NEW LOVING RELATIONSHIPS BOOK

It is not necessary to fight over money in your relationship. You can use a simple writing process to get clear on your negative thoughts about money. Write at the top of a clean sheet of paper: "My ten most negative thoughts about money are . . ." After listing your negative thoughts, take each one and convert it into a positive affirmation. You will immediately change your results with money.

You do have a relationship with money, you know. Its presence or absence strictly follows your thoughts. You can use it to beat yourself up (just as you can use a person to beat yourself up) if you want a little disapproval.

There is really no excuse to hang around in poverty. Give yourself approval and allow the money to flow your way. Remind yourself of what Rev. Ike once told me: *God is opulent.* So you either have a prosperity consciousness or a poverty consciousness.

Where do you begin to solve money conflicts? Each person must start by handling their own "money case." That includes all negative conditioning about money. You can take all kinds of seminars on money, read any number of books, and learn a whole range of things; but if you don't process your own emotional blocks about money, even those fine tools won't work. Some people actually have a "money rejection complex." It stems from a belief that money is somehow sinful or bad.

95

Money is not bad. Money is innocent. It is energy. Any other negative thought you have about it, you made up! Remember: only you can deprive yourself of anything.

John Randolph Price, author of *The Abundance Book*, explains that God does not provide us with money or homes—He gives of Himself. He gives us divine substance, and we turn that substance into money and homes by our thoughts. This substance flows through the mind of human beings and externalizes itself as a mirror of our thoughts. Money is a by-product of this process. We should focus on the cause, not the effect. You must have a relationship with this divine substance and you do that by having deep, profound gratitude.

Too often money is a taboo subject. I suggest regular, weekly meetings where partners discuss financial affairs, including current agreements, money goals, bills, future economic projects, savings, fears and feelings.

So if you are fighting about money, stop now! What good will that accomplish? And anyway, anger blocks money. Guilt blocks money.

I once mentioned to a friend who had taken the LRT that when we conduct the training we never mention the word *money* much, yet graduates frequently report that their incomes double after they take the training. When asked what he thought was the reason, he wrote this long letter:

All the money that anyone ever received came from other people. All the money that everyone ever spent went to other people. Money is a very pervasive substance and it pervades almost every relationship that you have. This is easy to see in the relationships you have with people you live with and share expenses with, and it is easy to see in the relationships with people you work with. However, even if your relationship is limited to meeting for dinner once a month to discuss Egyptian art, your question of who will pay for the dinner probably crosses your minds. Therefore, people tend to experience greater ease and abundance in their cash flow as they experience more ease and trust in their relationships. The LRT is based upon spiritual truth, the essence of which is the individual divinity of every person. The knowledge that you create your own reality by virtue of your personal divinity (as manifested by your ability to choose your thoughts and, in fact, change them at any time) brings the process of giving and receiving into present time. This means that patterns of obligations, guilt, and manipulation surrounding the giving and receiving of everything, including love and money, tend to drop away. For example, since I am a divine being, I have the thought of giving you something before I give it to you in every case. It follows that you must have the thought of receiving it before you do so. This makes receiving a causative act instead of a random accident over which you have no control. As long as you think that receiving obligates you or provides the giver the right to manipulate you, then it is safer to protect yourself from these unpleasant feelings by only giving, which seems to put you in control. Your willingness to receive is a service in itself; it allows the other person to give freely. For me, the LRT was a big step in learning to trust myself. The essence of prosperity consciousness is the unconditional willingness to trust the love and generosity of other people. For almost everyone, birth was our first experience of relationships with people whom we could see, and it probably taught us that it is painful to trust other people. A key element of parental conditioning subsequent to birth is that your parents' ideas are more trustworthy than your own. This is an idea that is enforced by most parents through the practices of reward and punishment that pervade any emotional system of logic that is based upon conditional love. Loving yourself is closely akin to trusting yourself, so that the increased self-esteem that graduates experience results in increased self-trust, which then results in an increased sense of financial abundance. Graduates of the LRT learn the art of receiving.

They remove the blocks to receiving love and money. There are tons of books on money, but the only one I am going to recommend is this one: *The Path to Wealth* by May McCarthy. It is a small book and it is spiritual. You don't need to read any other books on money after you read that one.

22. GETTING CLEAR ON SEX

I once worked with a couple that had been to many prominent sex clinics. While they were there, his sex "problem" (premature ejaculation) temporarily cleared up. But when they got home, it came back and they were on the verge of divorce again. I was leaving Los Angeles in 30 minutes, but when I got this call, I agreed to see him on my way to the airport. It was a shot in the dark. I made it very plain that I had very little time so he was going to have to answer my questions quickly and truthfully and he was going to have to trust me immediately. He agreed.

I went back to his first sexual experience. I found that his mother, who "knew" intuitively that *that* was going to be the night, yelled at him as he went out the door, "If you get a girl pregnant, I'll kill you!" For some reason he took it quite literally and he got the whole thing over quickly, so quickly that he did not get a chance to come inside the girl. He had never, however, made the connection between what his mother said and what happened. Being very embarrassed by his first sexual disaster, he decided there was something physically wrong with him, or even worse, something was perhaps wrong mentally. And then he could not perform again. I gave him a simple affirmation and asked him to promise to do it. He agreed. I asked him to write, "It is now safe for me to be inside of a woman," and "I am safe when I come inside a woman," etc. At the last minute I looked at his wife and said, "For some reason, I think you should also do an affirmation and the one I think you should do is this, "I am now willing for my husband to clear up his sex problem." She amazed me by saying, "How do you know me so well?" She confessed that she was afraid that if he cleared up his premature ejaculation he would start going out with other women. They wrote to me later saying that it worked.

Sexual problems are more complex than they may appear. Both parties are involved and it is important to find out how the patterns are intertwined. Sex "techniques" will never work permanently unless the necessary thoughts are changed.

Most of us could learn to receive a lot more pleasure than we are now experiencing. The key to this is your willingness to experience pleasure. To have a good sex life you must have high self-esteem. If you have a low opinion of yourself you won't think you deserve sexual pleasure. Another way of looking at this is to say that you will have only as much pleasure in sex as you are willing to allow yourself.

These days, people have read so much about sexual technique that both men and women are self-conscious and worried about gratifying their partners. What actually works best in bed is pleasing yourself. By this I mean that the partners can make an agreement to be responsible for their own orgasms by telling each other what is most pleasurable and taking turns in giving and receiving. If you agree to be completely honest about your desires and your responses, then there is never any need to wonder about whether your partner is happy or bored, satisfied or frustrated, tired or turned on.

Of course, sexual fulfillment requires you to get rid of all your old negative thoughts about sex being dirty, dangerous, forbidden, scary, or whatever. *Sex is innocent!* It is all those old negatives we attach to it that mess us up. You can start clearing them now by writing down all your negative thoughts about sex and turning them into affirmations.

This may seem obvious, but it is very important: When you are having sex, it helps to think about sex (many people actually think about the dry cleaning, the garbage, the kids, and the shopping instead). Focus your attention on the area of your body that is being touched. During foreplay when you are taking turns pleasuring each other, both people should concentrate their attention on the person receiving. You focus your attention on the area of his body being touched and your partner focuses his attention on the area of your body being touched; then you switch. Two minds focused on one body make very powerful sexual energy, and sex *is* energy. The purer your energy, the purer and greater the sexual experience.

It helps to remind yourself that you can stop and talk during a sexual experience—especially if it is not going the way you want. For some reason people behave as if, once they start, they can't change it or talk about it until it is over. Communication is important. You have to learn to ask for what you like.

Some people tend to hold their breath during love-making. Believe me, you can take in a lot more love if you are doing conscious breathing! And it is a wonderful time to do breathing together if you have learned how to do Liberation Breathing. Sex is totally different once you have resolved your birth trauma. For one thing, it suddenly becomes safe to let go totally; you can surrender because you know there is nothing lurking down there that is scary or sad. For another, your breathing is adjusted and you can handle a lot more energy and pleasure as a result.

With sex, all that matters, according to *A Course in Miracles* is this: Are you in the ego's thought system with sex or the Holy Spirit's thought system? If you are in the latter, then it will be a sacred holy experience. As Bhagwan Rajneesh has said: "The primal energy of sex has the reflection of God in it. Sex is divine." It is the energy that creates new life. Therefore, you should accept sex with joy and acknowledge its sacredness. When a man approaches his wife, he should have a sacred feeling, as if he were going to a temple. As a wife goes to her husband, she should be full of the reverence one has nearing God. Orgasm is for the momentary realization of *Samadhi.* The ego vanishes. Orgasm is a state of self-effacement. This is the reason we are attracted to it.

In Tantric teachings, sexual love represents sacrament; its ultimate goal is union with God. There are even books on how you and your mate can use tantric sex to achieve physical immortality! (*New Age Tantra* by John Zitko, 1985)

Immortals can tell the difference between the "old sex" and the "new sex." They experience old sex before they understood the concept of physical immortality and worked out their death urge. (Some may actually be afraid they will die if they really let go. An immortal would never have that thought.) The old sex was practiced before one had worked out one's birth trauma. If you have not released your birth trauma, it could come up during sex and cause fear and withholding. After working out the death urge and the birth trauma, one feels safe enough to handle more energy in the body without the unconscious fear of death. Immortals also know how to use sex for rejuvenation. They work with the breath.

The space a couple chooses for lovemaking should be like a temple. I recommend having an altar in the room. I recommend playing soft music, especially Indian classical music because of its very high frequency. There should be fresh flowers, candles, beautiful objects and soothing fabrics around. Everything in the room should be beautiful to you. Television, library books, computers, stacks of stuff and old bedding are not conducive to romance and holiness. Doing a simple puja, or worship at the altar beforehand will put you in the right frame of mind—even doing something as simple as waving a lit incense stick before photos of holy ones is good. Then, turn the experience over to God.

Think very carefully about your lover. Some teachers will tell you that there can be karmic exchange through sexual activity. Sex is not a simple matter of connecting and disconnecting. Some say that the linking that results from one single sexual activity may last for approximately fourteen months on higher planes and that the karmic link lasts as well. So, think about the consequences of who you sleep with. If you are doing breathwork and purifying yourself, you certainly don't want to have sex with someone who is angry and take on his or her case and karma! Think about the consequences before you sleep with someone tonight who may have slept with someone else last night. Do you really want to take on all those energies? Sleeping with multiple partners can have karmic as well as bodily consequences. It is important to think about "safe sex" on both a physical and spiritual level.

23. **HANDLING JEALOUSY**

Fred and Barbara were always fighting about jealousy. She claimed Fred was always interested in other women and paying more attention to them than to her. She said she wanted a divorce because Fred was now interested in her best friend. Fred had had one affair but stopped it when she threatened divorce. At first it looked as though Fred was the culprit all around. She was sure of it, of course. But when I explored their cases with more depth, I found out that Barbara had a sister of whom she was insanely jealous. This sister seemed to win all the attention from their father and Barbara claimed that her father not only paid more attention to her sister than he did to her, but he also gave this sister more gifts and money. Furthermore, this sister seemed to have a way with men; and men who came to visit the family always flirted with her sister instead of her. So what Barbara had done was set up a situation where Fred became her father and all these "other women" became her sister. Then she would go into a rage, and who she was *really* angry with was her father. And when she felt like "killing" the other woman, she really felt like killing her own sister. Fred thought that women were out to trap him. Because of Barbara's insane jealousy and possessiveness, he was sure of it. She fit his pattern. She was like his mother who was always possessive of him. Once they saw they were trapped in patterns and that they were unconsciously trying to heal each other of old family conditions, things lightened up. Barbara finally forgave her sister and got rid of her resentment by discovering her own beauty and talents. Fred stopped acting out her pattern and belief systems. He confessed he really didn't want any other woman anyway. When he forgave his mother for being so possessive, Barbara also stopped acting out his belief systems and she stopped being overly possessive.

I have observed that the more you raise your self-esteem, the less jealousy you will have. People with high self-esteem feel centered and confident most of the time, and they know that they can be happy even when they are alone. They are aware that they can be happy without their current partner and that they can create for themselves a new and better partner if the current one goes

SONDRA RAY & MARKUS RAY

away. People with high self-esteem know that they can get what they want, and they usually set up their lives so that there is little room for jealousy.

When somebody asked me how to handle jealousy, I suggested that they start by looking at why they set up a jealousy situation in the first place. In other words, what is the payoff? Are they using jealousy scenes to beat themselves up? Why do they want misery in their lives? If you find that another person is involved with the one you love, ask yourself these questions:

1. Did I attract this situation to prove I wasn't good enough?

2. Does the other woman represent my sister who got more of my father's love?

3. Does the other man represent my brother who got more of my mother's love?

4. Was my relationship getting too good and too close, so that I had to destroy it?

5. Was I getting more love than I thought I deserved, so that I had to get rid of it?

6. Am I addicted to pain, and do I secretly love it?

7. Do I think misery is the natural state?

8. Am I hooked on drama instead of peace?

9. Am I trying to prove that others are out to get me?

10. Do I think that I can never trust a man (or woman), and this proves it? Do I think I can't get what I want?

11. Do I think life is a rip-off, and this proves it?

12. Do I think I can't keep what I want?

13. Am I using this mess so that I have an excuse to get rid of my partner?

14. Do I love to punish myself with this because I have guilt about something?

15. Do I secretly want to have other partners myself, and am I lying to myself?

16. Am I trying to get rid of my partner?

Do you begin to see why you can't blame others for your jealousy? You created this mess! You wanted it to prove something; you wanted to prove that your negative beliefs were right. Remember: *What you believe to be true, you create.*

24. UNDERSTANDING

EMOTIONAL INCEST

Jill told me that she and George had started out with a fabulous sex life, but as soon as they had gotten married, she suddenly got "turned off." She blamed George, but none of her reasons seemed to make sense. She finally admitted that. I asked her if this had happened before and she confessed that it happened with another man, and she noticed that the situation did not arise until they had moved in together. "And what was common about both of these men?" I asked her.

"They each look like my father," she replied.

I pointed out that since these men were so much like her father, it was hard for her to let herself stay turned on to them because it would be like having incest. Why, she wanted to know, was she able to make love to them in the beginning then?

She had a hard time accepting this explanation at first because she did not want to believe that she could have been sexually attracted to her father. She agreed to take the training and she repeated it several times. After she did the processes concerning incest and heard others talk about their feelings, she felt safe enough to let some of those memories come up. Even so, she did not believe it until her fourth training when she suddenly let out a loud outburst of rage and started shaking and seemed about to faint. At that moment, she got in touch with the anger she felt at not being able to make love to her father! This emotional release healed her and the problem cleared up.

I have always thought it would be unethical to avoid the topic of emotional incest in a relationship course. My research in this area has taught me that suppressed incestuous feelings affect most people's sex lives to such a degree that emotional incest underlies many of the problems that arise. Jill's question was a good one. I used to wonder why couples so often start out with a great sex life, only to find it less and less pleasurable after living together or getting married. You would think that as couples got closer and closer, their sex life would improve. The fact is that in the beginning of a relationship any incestuous feelings are very deeply suppressed. However, after a couple sets up housekeeping, childhood experiences are unconsciously recreated and the mate becomes more and more like the parent we once lived with. The more the mate becomes like the parent, the less one is able to make love to him. As this unconscious connection gets stronger, we are less able to make love to them because of the taboo against making love to one of your parents. Often it takes a few years for this to occur because it takes a lot of energy and love and emotion to push up suppressed material from the unconscious.

Many people "go unconscious" during the incest processes of their first LRT. They have such a charge on this area that they are afraid to look at it. Slowly they realize that the things they can't talk about are the things that run them, but sometimes people are in their third training before they allow themselves to recall incestuous feelings. There is a lot of unnecessary guilt about incestuous feelings.

You must remember that as a baby you were a very tactile, sensual being who got touched all the time. Bathing was a time of particular pleasure where you got touched all over your body, including your genitals. Also remember that your parents were then in their sexual prime. As an infant, you found this touching wonderful, but one day it suddenly stopped without explanation. Your mind probably got stuck at some point when the family sexual energy got too strong and everyone shut down.

What can you do about this pattern now? Examine your feelings about your parents and your brothers and sisters and acknowledge whatever you find. Forgive yourself for letting this pattern run your life. People who have told the truth about family sexuality in our group sessions have felt totally liberated and often later report wonderful changes in their lovemaking. In the LRT we have special processes to release suppressed incestuous feelings. In the meantime, it will be very helpful to you just to "see" that you may have your partner set up to be a substitute parent, and therefore your sex life with him or her may be blocked.

In therapy, psychologists have what they call "The Madonna/Prostitute Complex." For example, a man cannot get an erection with his wife but he has no trouble getting one with a prostitute. This freaks him out, so he goes into therapy. Any good therapist would point out that he has his wife set up as his mother (emotional incest) but the prostitute is not placed in that "mind set" — so sex "works" with her.

25. KNOWING THE PURPOSE OF YOUR RELATIONSHIP

I never thought much about having a purpose until I went to an enlightened business school for entrepreneurs. The first thing the teacher did was to establish the purpose of the school. Since we were the first graduating class, that seemed appropriate. It was also a practice session, because we agreed the most important thing in creating a new business is for the people involved to know the purpose for the business. And they all should agree. And everyone should know what each word means when the purpose is written down. We thought it was going to be easy. It took us days and days. This made me think a lot about purpose.

I never used to think about what I was doing in a relationship or why I was in one and not another. I never bothered to create a purpose for my relationship. It took a lot of years to understand that a great purpose for having a relationship was to gain enlightenment. In other words, we are together for the evolution of our souls. That is a great purpose. It changes everything when you put your relationship in that context. If I am here in this relationship to help my mate evolve and if he is here in this relationship to help me evolve, then a whole new world opens up for us.

This realization gives a new aliveness to the relationship. This makes one become more alert. This realization brings meaning to everything we experience together.

I now call my husband my "ascension buddy." In other words, his presence makes me go up the ladder of holiness. His presence makes me go to a higher frequency and vice versa. This is something you should establish at the beginning. The way you conceive a relationship is very important. Don't wait to talk about these things down the road.

Do it at the beginning. *A Course in Miracles* talks about the difference between a holy relationship and an unholy one. I have paraphrased the basic concepts here:

An unholy relationship is based on differences, where each one thinks the other has what he has not.

They come together, each to complete himself and rob the other. They stay until they think there is nothing left to steal, and then they move on. And so they wander through the world as strangers . . .

A holy relationship starts from a different premise.

Each one has looked within and seen no lack. Accepting his completion, he would extend it by joining with another, whole as himself . . . this relationship has Heaven's holiness. How far from home can a relationship so like to Heaven be?

Think of what a holy relationship can teach. If both of you agree to commit your friendship to "something greater" than each of you, you will have tremendous spiritual force backing you up.

26. TREATING EACH OTHER WITH UTMOST KINDNESS

My parents agreed never to raise their voices in the presence of us girls. It was a wonderful agreement and I benefited so much from the absence of anger. I only saw them treating each other kindly in our home.

But I never saw how they solved issues as they did that behind closed doors. I was kind of a gifted "channel" as a kid and sometimes my Mom would ask me questions. One day when she came out of their bedroom, I saw her crying. I realized that they had in fact had an argument. On that day, she asked me a very, very difficult question. She asked me this: "Why is it that people who love each other the most often treat each other the worst? I was unable to answer her question. I found myself speechless as this question was way over my head. I was only five years old, and could not speak; but I always remembered that question. Decades later my Mom took the LRT from me and I told her in front of everyone. "Mom this training is the answer to your question."

As I grew up and traveled around the world, I was in many homes where it appeared the family members hated each other. They seemed out to get each other. It seemed like they couldn't wait to put each other down. It seemed like they would just as soon beat each other up. It seemed like their favorite way to communicate was to be sarcastic or to yell. I could never understand this. And then one day I read that most murders are committed in the home! I was appalled. I went to a home one day where the only one that got treated decently was the dog! I always wondered why this was, just as my mother had wondered.

The research we have done for the LRT has shed some light. Most people are angry at their parents and they are taking it out on their mates. They aren't even relating to the person they are living with. They are relating to someone the person is set up to be. When you clean up this anger with your parents (and you need to do this whether they are dead or alive), then you can start relating to your mate as a friend that you will treat like an angel.

Meditate on the idea of treating your mate and family members as if they were honored guests, kings and queens. Isn't that how you would like to be treated? Meditate on the idea of treating him or her like a saint. See the divinity in everyone and then they will start acting divine around you. If you really love your mate, don't they deserve to be treated like an honored guest? Think about it. Can you do it?

27. HAVING THE RIGHT ATTITUDE

A wonderful little book, *The Door of Everything*, channeled by Ruby Nelson, talks about the "Ascension" attitudes. These attitudes will bring you good relationships, and they will thrust you into an altogether fabulous life. The Ascension attitudes are *Love*, *Praise* and *Gratitude*. If your being radiates these attitudes, you will easily attract all the wonderful friends and mates you could ever want.

Giving thanks for the good things you have always brings you more good things. Many people spend time focusing on what they don't have. Every time I have focused on a lack for any length of time it has led me into misery.

Catherine Ponder, in discussing the principle of giving thanks, says that your highest good is there for you, even if you are not experiencing it yet. I repeat: If you want a mate, say this: "I am so happy and grateful that my perfect mate is here now." God is ready when you are.

The Source thrives on having you receive from it, because the giver always expands by the giving. So don't block the things you deserve to receive and don't block the love that is there for you. In the same way, if you lose something, know that it was no longer best for you, and that the Source is clearing the way to give you something even greater.

If you focus on loss you'll experience more loss. If you give thanks for what you have, you'll get more.

I always try to have the attitude that whatever happens is the perfect thing to happen. Even if it seems "bad" at first, I always know there is a lesson and it probably happened so I could receive the lesson. I always manage to turn everything into a "win." I never lose this attitude, and I stay happy.

So, do you have an attitude of gratitude at all times? Writing in a "gratitude journal" keeps you in the flow of appreciation. For about a year Markus and I would write 10 things a day we were grateful for in our journals. It kept us in the right mindset for things to flow to us naturally. And when they did not, to look at ourselves and see the thoughts we needed to "let go of."

28. HAVING A SPIRITUAL

MISSION TOGETHER

Imagine what would happen if couples sat down and decided from the beginning what kind of mission they were going to accomplish together for the world—*and they actually did it!* This spiritual mission could be a joint career that is high in service. But if they were already in different careers, they could still decide what kind of service they could offer the world apart from their jobs.

When people are deeply in love, they feel a natural concern for the state of the world and they want to do something about it. If love has waned and the relationship is stale, it might be due to the couple never acting together on that sense of purpose. It is never too late to infuse your marriage or relationship with this gift. It is not only a gift to the world, but a gift to the relationship; it gives the relationship true meaning.

I have studied successful relationships of partners who were equally powerful. In fact the equality in the relationship was part of the success.

They are able to handle the power of an equal relationship by focusing on something greater than themselves. In an article called "100 Ways to Fix the World," the author interviewed one hundred famous people and asked for their recommendation. Filmmaker Eleanor Coppola said: "Every seven years, every able-bodied soul should do three months of public service." This is a good idea. If you are single, you might meet a wonderful partner doing that. I think, however, that service should be more often than that.

Missions are satisfying. Finding my mission felt like the true beginning of my life. Everything before that was anticlimactic. I consider it a past life. When I tell people what I was doing before I accepted this mission, they cannot believe that I am the same person. I did nursing which was of course also a great service.

Once I held a class where each student was to select an act of service that was a big *stretch* for them. I told them this would force them to grow and they would become greater. Almost everyone totally underestimated their abilities. They could not seem to stretch at all. They were somehow afraid of expansion. What are you doing to stretch yourself? What is the mission you can be committed to?

29. MAKE YOUR LIVING SPACE THE BEST FOR YOUR RELATIONSHIP

Does your environment at home support your relationship in the highest way?

People often laugh at how adamant I am about neatness in regard to their space. Yes

I am a Virgo and I know that neatness affects your mind and your relationship. When I visit someone's home I can instantly determine—by the way the home looks—a family's "aliveness quotient "and how much they respect each other. This is not a matter of finances or expensive items. The way you care for your living space reflects how you feel about yourself and those you live with. Your home and the various spaces that comprise it offer a clear, tangible way to measure your level of self-esteem and vitality.

Let's take the kitchen!
* Is the stove dirty and are the cooking pots banged up with handles missing?
* Is the food in the refrigerator moldy?
* Are the cupboards a mess?
* Are the sponges in the sink dirty and are dirty dishes stacked up?
* Is there birdseed all over the floor?
* Is the garbage overflowing?

Let's take the living room!
* Are the plants dead?
* Have the cats scratched up the furniture?
* Are the light bulbs burned out?
* Is the TV dominating everything?
* Is it a mess?

Let's take the bathroom!
* Are the towels rancid?
* Is the shower curtain moldy and is the mirror spotted?
* Do the shower and bathtub have dirty rings?

❖ Are old empty shampoo bottles stacked up?

❖ Is the bathroom scale rusty?

❖ Is there grime?

Let's take the bedroom:

❖ Is your bedroom an office and not conducive to romance?

❖ Is junk piled around with boxes of items that are not being used?

❖ Is the bed always unmade and are sheets not changed?

❖ Are the closets bulging with old clothes that are not flattering, or are clothes too small?

❖ Can you get turned on in there or not?

❖ Why not throw open your closets and try everything on? Then look in the mirror and ask yourself if you like what you see . . . does it turn you on? If the answer is no, give it away. (How do you expect your partner to be turned on if you aren't?) Always dressing nicely, even at home, enhances your mood and sensuality. I live with an artist so I try to look my best every day. It is one way you can show appreciation to your mate. Show you care about his or her experience of you.

What about your car?

❖ Is it banged up?

❖ Is the outside dirty most of the time?

❖ Is dog and cat hair everywhere on the seats?

❖ Are there cigarette butts, gum wrappers, and soda cans around?

❖ Are there old newspapers and piles of crap on the floor of the car?

❖ Are major parts of the car not working well?

❖ Is it an old wreck?

❖ What does it say about the way you feel about your body?

And what about your yard?

❖ Is it untidy and un-kept? Does it make you happy to look at it?

❖ Are the flower beds weeded?

❖ Have you mowed the grass?

Naturally you want to feel relaxed in your own home and not uptight. I realize that. But notice the difference in your mood and the vitality of your relationship when your space is pretty and neat. Maybe you need to hire a housekeeper once a week or once every two weeks. They will keep the grime from building up. Mine only charges $130! Some people clean surfaces but leave the grime underneath. If that is you, have you ever stopped to consider that grime, dirt, filth, junk and things falling apart is part of your death urge?

I have never understood why people don't fix things immediately instead of letting them go. When you don't fix something right away, you end up with a disintegrating and broken down place. In time, it will become depressing and then you will feel too overwhelmed to tackle it. If you wait to handle things, things will be run down.

On the other hand, careful continual maintenance of your place and belongings creates a cycle of positive energy for you. When your mind is clear and your thoughts are orderly, you will want every little thing fixed. When you fix things, your relationship improves.

A couple has to negotiate and work out their own way of doing household chores—a way that truly works for both partners. This can get tricky if one grew up in a house where everything was very neat and the other grew up in a house of "hoarders." Habits learned in childhood can be a big bone of contention—but solutions can always be found. Chores don't have to cause tension.

I once lived with a man who was neater than I was! If you know me, this is hard to believe since I have always had very fastidious habits. He however was an extreme perfectionist. You could not even leave one coffee cup in the sink nor one fingerprint on the glass coffee table. I started feeling nervous around him. In my eyes, he was "obsessed."

I wondered if he had a rough toilet training! Several times I felt like criticizing him for being so extreme. Fortunately, I did not. I had a brain storm. I decided to set him down and interview him and ask him what his "mind set" was on this subject. So I did that one Sunday morning and his response shocked me. "Well, Sondra," he said. "It is really very simple: Prepare every room for God." I was speechless and quickly I decided to go up to his thought. I asked him to train me to be like him. He did and I got the blessing.

Years later his training created a miracle for me. There was a fire in my apartment building in Marina del Rey, Ca. I was not home at the time. All the apartments were ruined and when I came home I saw that the walls in the hall were like black tar and the paintings were melted into the walls. The wreath on my door had melted into the door.

As I reluctantly put the key in the door, I said to Babaji, my guru, "Well I don't care about my furniture, but I hope my sacred art is somehow okay." I entered my apt and there was not one speck of soot anywhere. Mine was the only apartment not touched. My neighbors lost everything. How could that be? Because I was impeccable and furthermore I had altars in every room.

30. CREATING A SACRED PARTNERSHIP

A personal relationship is a sacred responsibility. It should not be based on physical, intellectual or emotional attraction alone. Such a partnership must be based on a commitment to manifest the highest and the best in one another.

In a sacred partnership, each partner is equally committed to assisting the other in his or her spiritual growth. Each must understand that the most profound reason they are together is for the evolution of their souls.

This creates a whole new vibration between them.

A relationship should be about growth and movement. It should create a holy, interpersonal environment for the evolution of two souls. A relationship is a process. In that process, the couple should celebrate changes in themselves which are stimulated by one another. They should not resent the fact that the mate is encouraging them to change. Each should want the other to become all that he or she can be and should not feel threatened by this desire. In other words, you should not hold yourself back in any way, nor should you allow the other to hold you back. In fact, you should use the support of your mate to help propel you forward, to advance. Each should enjoy empowering the other, but neither should give away his or her power. Don't sell out—work it out!

I am describing intimacy as a path. Strive for intimacy instead of intensity because intimacy leads to transformation. The power of intimacy brings up all one's fears to be processed. You must first want to become enlightened so you can make the relationship work for you. Then you must eliminate all barriers to expressing your love.

Beware of using a special relationship as a substitute for God. *A Course in Miracles* says that "a special relationship is the ego's chief weapon to keep you from God" (See next chapter.) So, if you are spending all your time and energy (as most people do) trying to make the relationship work with someone who you think is more special than you or anyone else—it will never work.

I am talking about a paradigm where two partners are striving for the spiritual adventure of exploring together the higher possibilities of Spirit. Ask yourself: "Am I willing to go for that?

31. HOLY VERSUS UNHOLY

RELATIONSHIPS

I always encourage everyone to read *A Course in Miracles* and to keep reading it as a life-long spiritual path. All answers are in that book!

This chapter will summarize what the Course's teachings say on the subject of relationships. The Course explains that in a special relationship, we regard one individual as more "special" than anyone else, more valuable than ourselves and even more precious than God! But this idea is a delusion. As children of God, all human beings together comprise the Sonship. In coveting a special relationship with one human being, we limit our love to only one small segment of the Sonship, and are inevitably aware that we have forsaken the totality of that Sonship. This brings guilt into our relationship, and guilt houses fear. The "special love relationship" is a compelling distraction we use to obscure our attraction to God the Father. In other words, within the special relationship, we deny our need for God by substituting the need for special people and special things. Hope for salvation depends solely on one individual, and so the attention our partner may devote to activities outside the relationship feels like a threat to our wellbeing. Because special relationships delude us into believing that they can offer salvation, we also accept the erroneous idea that separation is salvation. In fact, such exclusive relationships serve as the ego's chief weapon in barring us from a Heavenly existence here.

An unholy relationship feeds on differences; each partner perceives that his mate possesses qualities or attributes he doesn't possess. On the surface, such a partnership seems to bear out the old claim that "opposites attract." Upon closer inspection, however, a different picture emerges. In reality, each partner enters into such a union with the idea of completing himself or herself and robbing the other. They each remain in the relationship only until they decide that there is nothing left to steal, and then they move on.

With these kinds of relationships, whatever reminds a person of past grievances attracts them. I call this "being attracted to your patterns."

It's obvious these partners aren't there out of a wish to join with their mate in Spirit. More surprising, however is the fact that they aren't even attempting to join with the body of their mate. Instead, they seek a union with the bodies of those *who are not there!* (paraphrase Text, p331) such as their father or mother or others. Based on these impulses, this unholy bond has little to do with real love. This attempt at union ultimately excludes the very person with whom the partnership was made.

The special love relationship also has a flip side. In the special hate relationship, negative impulses are merely more transparent, for the relationship is clearly one of anger and attack. In this arrangement, one person becomes the focus of our anger; we hold onto everything they have done to hurt us. The special hate relationship wreaks vengeance on the past. It holds the past against us (text, pg. 322) and it involves a great amount of pain, anxiety, despair, guilt, and attack.

Every special relationship you have made is a substitute for God's will and glorifies your own instead. Every special relationship harms you by occupying your mind so completely that you cannot hear the call of Truth.

The relationship is based on the assumption that something within us is lacking and therefore we have special needs. To satisfy these needs, we come to believe that another individual is capable of giving us what is missing in ourselves. A conviction of our own littleness lies at the heart of every special relationship, for when two mates endeavor to become one entity they've forgotten the presence of God in their relationship. Rather than augmenting the relationship, this diminishes its greatness.

In sharp contrast to the special relationship, a "holy relationship" rests on solid ground. Each partner has looked within himself and perceives nothing inherent lacking. Accepting his own completion, he finds pleasure in extending it, and so joins with another person who is also whole. Because they have both evolved to the same degree, no great differences exist between them. This relationship contains and reflects Heaven's holiness.

Completion comes from union with God and from the extension of that union to others. As such, a holy partnership mirrors the rich relationship between the Son of God and his Father; it has the power to alleviate all suffering. In such a partnership, sin cannot exist since God Himself has arranged each holy union in accordance with His own plan.

The Holy Spirit knows we have made special relationships which He will not take away. But He would convert them from unholy to holy relationships if we allow that. A holy relationship requires that both partners strive toward a common goal. When two people share the same intent and they search for the love of God, a healing takes place. Giving flows endlessly. No wants or needs hinder it, for in giving of themselves, both are blessed. Moreover, these blessings flourish and extend to others.

A light emanates outward, illuminating the world. In a holy relationship, seemingly difficult situations are accepted as blessings. Instead of obsessively criticizing one's partner, forever pointing out any imperfections that must be changed or discarded, there is a pull toward praise and appreciation. Having created an atmosphere of love, each partner may begin to receive the Christ in each other.

32. MARRIAGE

Many jokes about marriage are very sad instead of funny.

A lady has finished a meal in a hotel coffee shop and asks for her check. Surprised, the waitress exclaims.

"But I put your breakfast on the tab of the man sitting next to you, the guy who just left."

"What made you do that?" the lady asks, "I don't even know him. I have never seen that man before in my life"

"I am sorry," the waitress explains, "You two weren't talking to each other, so I thought you were married."

This joke reveals an all-too-common phenomenon. Did you know that a psychologist once interviewed 40,000 married couples on communication patterns and it turned out they talked to each other on the average only *27 minutes* a week? Why does marriage so often leave two people alienated from one another? I have been investigating this question for years.

Once I found a book by Bhagawan Rajneesh who declared that marriage is out of date and that is destroys all possibilities of happiness. He insisted that marriage makes everyone a zoo animal, that it exacerbates the will to die and leads to prostitution! He proposed that marriage is an anachronistic barrier that must disappear and that it has ruined the status of women! Wow, that really stirred me up.

Over time, I studied the subject more and deeply, reading other spiritual books such as Swami Kryananda's *How to Spiritualize Your Marriage*, which advocated marriage for another set of reasons. Gradually I began to feel that the institution of marriage itself was not so negative. At fault were the false notions about what marriage should mean and the way people responded to one another once inside the marriage. In other words, marriage becomes a sacred bond only if it is made sacred—otherwise it is simply a social contract. Sound reasons for getting married that I read and thought about included these:

- ❖ Marriage can help a person achieve inner balance (especially between reason and feeling).
- ❖ Marriage helps break the confines of selfishness and the ego, teaching one to live in a larger reality than one's own.

❖ Marriage helps one expand one's identity.

❖ Marriage helps break the confines of selfishness and the ego, teaching one to live in a larger reality than one's own.

❖ Marriage provides a "proving ground" for one's inner spiritual development. It tests ones spiritual qualities.

❖ Marriage is a vehicle through which one can achieve union with God (after achieving union with God in your mate).

Pushing ahead, I began looking into Yogananda's teachings on marriage and came across this piece of wisdom: "The desire for marriage is universal because of the cosmic power of love to draw everything back to oneness." He stresses how important it is that marriage be based on divine friendship between equals with unconditional love, unconditional loyalty, and the divine qualities of kindness, respect, trust and faith. He prioritized the essential foundations for marriage in this way:

1. Soul unity (similar spiritual ideals and goals and a willingness to attain them through study and self-discipline.

2. Similarity of interests.

3.   Physical attraction (which soon loses its attractive power if soul unity and similarity of interests are not present).

How often people reverse these priorities and suffer because of it! Here is a chart I made up of the two bases of marriage:

EGO-BASED RELATIONSHIP GOVERNED BY:	SPIRIT-BASED RELATIONSHIP GOVERNED BY:
Separation	Oneness
Conflict	Love
Fear	Safety
Pain	Peace
Anger	Harmony
Worry	Certainty
Misery	Perfect Health
Scarcity	Abundance
Depression	Happiness
Aging	Longevity
Death	More Aliveness

Clearly, marriage is no panacea. It is not usually true that things will clear up and get better if you are married. Marriage can accentuate all problems. But if marriage is manifested in a spiritual context and each partner is willing to work on themselves, it does not have to become stagnant.

Is the marriage going to lead to liberation or delusion? That is why you need to know the difference between a holy relationship and an unholy relationship.

33. RAISING A CHILD OF GOD

If you are planning to have children in the future, there is a fascinating book called *The Child of Your Dreams* by Laura Huxley. It should be read long before conception. She asserts that when conceiving, a spiritually compatible couple has the ability to attract highly spiritual souls. Before conception you can send out an invitation to the kind of child you want. In meditation, you welcome the child but much preparation needs to be done to purify oneself. The next book I recommend would be *The Secret Life of the Unborn Child* by Dr. Thomas Verny. It is all about prenatal psychology. After that,

I recommend *Ideal Birth* written by me

Birth Without Violence by Dr. Leboyer

Birth Reborn by Dr. Odont

These four books will get you started. The last one I am going to recommend is *How to Raise a Child of God* by my husband, Markus's teacher, Tara Singh.

During the last decade remarkable headway has been made in the field of pre-and perinatal psychology. One of the most significant findings shows that imprints for tendencies toward dysfunctional behavior in childhood and adulthood are actually formed as early as in the womb, from conception to birth and in the first twelve months. This contradicts the previously accepted theory that these imprints develop when the child is one to three years old.

Children with reduced prenatal birth and perinatal trauma are generally brighter, more alert, intuitive, assertive, and creative. They exhibit independent learning patterns, are clearer about their own needs, display high self-esteem and score measurably higher on IQ tests.

Child rearing is a trying yet fascinating process. I like to remind parents that "Children are you gurus." Youngsters unflinchingly act out the subconscious thoughts of the parents. It is unnerving to realize children are acting out your subconscious minds. But if you study their behavior and look at yourself because of it, you will learn a great deal. It is very wise to take careful note of what they are doing and saying and ask yourself what it says about you.

One must also remember that children are already developed souls from their own past lives. Because children come as guests to their family, one should honor the knowledge they arrive with. As Roger Woolger tells us in the book *Other Lives Other Selves*, a child is not a blank slate at birth. Nor can we delude ourselves into thinking that they have to learn everything from us, or that they are simply helpless creatures. The true meaning of education is "drawing out" by bringing forth the wisdom our children already possess, not by imposing our own will upon them.

Tara Singh offers exceptional advice in the book *How to Raise a Child of God:*

The child is born with his own space and with his own resources.

It is the responsibility of the parent not to intrude on that innocence.

The function of the parent is to awaken a child to his own eternity, in his own holiness, to the perfection of what God created.

A child needs to play; mental faculties must awaken in their own internal way and should never be forced. If he is protected from being imposed upon, he

will have the discrimination of his own convictions and will not violate what is true within.

It would be so good if you could take your children to a prayer or mediation room in your house . . . a spacious little room uncluttered, with a few cushions, a bowl of water, a plant, and a picture or two of Divine Beings. This room can be alive with purity of space. Take your child into this room every day and come to peace within yourselves.

Here are more of Tara Singh's lovely teachings:

Teach your child not skills, but love to share.

Teach him to have more space in his life, the richness of stillness.

Teach him to widen gaps of silence between the thoughts with relaxation.

Teach him that all things in their origin are of the one Source.

Teach him to pray for his adversary to regain his own peace and harmony.

Teach him not to be controlled by another.

Teach him to bless all things with his peace.

Teach him non-waste and the love of conservation; teach him to be a friend of trees, dawn and twilight.

Teach him simplicity and gratefulness. To love virtue.

Teach him to be a friend unto himself.

The purpose of parenthood is to return the child to God. To raise a child of God is to allow God to participate in their upbringing. Would you like to make the civilization really great? Would you like your children to actualize that dream? Then teach your children this: *Thought is Creative.*

Negative thoughts produce negative results and positive thoughts produce positive results. Teach them to apply this truth to every aspect of their life. (Why didn't we learn that the first day of school?)

Always set an example of this by constantly raising the quality of your own thoughts.

34. DEVOTION: A COUPLE WORSHIPPING TOGETHER

When we worship, we "revere the worth of" something or someone. Worship is natural, the highest, most nonjudgmental form of love, and to refrain from it is unnatural. When we worship a person, we see no wrong in him whatsoever. We open ourselves completely to him. If we worship a teacher or Master, we will learn very quickly, for we will be open and receptive to all he has to say. To receive our brother's wisdom, we must pay careful attention to the way in which we worship, for discriminatory worship leads us down a meaningless path. Instead, we should worship all of life and feel the very best we can. Through worship we contribute to a more advanced civilization.

Once you clarify your own ideas about worship, which may have been muddled by traditional religious perspectives, you can then start over with a fresh perspective on worship and devotion. Create your own forms and your own altar honoring your most sacred feelings.

Devotions cleanse our being and bring us nearer to the Holy Spirit. Here are some suggested devotions you can do with your partner. They will enhance your relationship and your life if you do them together:

- ❖ Do Breathwork
- ❖ Read *A Course in Miracles* together aloud to each other
- ❖ Chant mantras
- ❖ Meditate
- ❖ Write affirmations
- ❖ Fast
- ❖ Appreciate silence
- ❖ Pray out loud or in silence
- ❖ Fire purification
- ❖ Visit holy places
- ❖ Listen to spiritual music
- ❖ Do a sweat lodge
- ❖ Attend seminars
- ❖ Spread enlightenment and networking

- ❖ Commit to a Peace Project
- ❖ For brave couples—Shave your heads (best done at the ashram)
- ❖ Keep a daily journal of gratitude
- ❖ Read enlightened books

The holy relationship offers many opportunities to appreciate your mate. Are you? Doing spiritual practices together gives you the chance to "revere the worth" of your Creator, and by doing this together you are "revering the worth" of your mate. See our book called *Spiritual Intimacy: What You Really Want With A Mate.* We lay out many practices that will bring you more communion with each other.

The old adage, "The family that prays together stays together," is still very true. A person, a couple, or a family need to have a daily practice that gives each a sense of inner peace and harmony, in order for their home to be a sanctuary of Love, not a den of differences and conflict. A practice in the spiritual life of worship, kept very simple and true, based on self-introspection and self-correction, as well as mutual adoration and praise, lifts you up and those around you. Why don't you try reading one chapter out of this book together with your mate, or family members? Then discuss it. See what happens!

35. HANDLING KARMIC

DEBTS AND DUES

Understanding the laws of reincarnation and karma contributes immeasurably to the process of emotional clearing.

The spiritual master Paramahansa Yogananda says, "Reincarnation is the progress of a soul through many lives on the earth plane, as through so many grades in a school, before it graduates to the immortal perfection of oneness with God."

He also says that in order to comprehend the justification of man's apparent inequalities, we must first understand the law of reincarnation.

Knowledge of this law was lost in the West during the Dark Ages. Yogananda says Jesus spoke of this law when He said, "Elias is come already; and they knew him not" (Elias reincarnated as John the Baptist).

Yogananda points out that, without reincarnation, there would be no Divine justice operating for those souls who have not yet had a chance to express themselves, such as a baby born dead. (Yogananda 1982).

If there were no law of cause and effect in the physical world, all would be chaos.

The Master Meher Baba says this:

> "All that has happened in past lives does have its own unconscious, but effective, share in determining one's actions and responses in this life. Fate is really man's own creation pursuing him from past lives. Karmic determination is the condition of true responsibility. It means that an individual will reap what he sows. According to karmic law he can neither avoid the debts or the dues. It is through his own binding karma that he invites upon himself pleasure or pain. He keeps re-incarnating to pay off his debts and recover his dues. But even then, he may be unable to clear his account for two reasons.

> 1.   All the persons with whom he or she has karmic links may not be incarnate when he has taken a body.

2.   *Due to particular limitations of his capacities or circumstances, he or she may not be able to meet all the complex circumstances. He may even go on adding to his debts and dues (i.e., creating new karma). The result could be that there is difficulty getting out of his complex karmic entanglements.*

These entanglements would be endless if there were no provisions for release. The help of a perfect master is enormous for this. The perfect Master can bring emancipation. (Now you know why I am always trying to get people to Babaji!). Another way out is spiritual purification and service to humanity." (*Discourses pp. 334-337*)

If you meet someone new and you feel instantly repulsed by him or her, perhaps you share some bad karma. If you meet someone new and you experience instant camaraderie, perhaps you have shared wonderful past lives with this person. The same dynamic holds true for countries.

What parts of the world have you always wanted to visit? Are there other parts you would never want to visit?

Recently Markus and I have had several clients who had very stuck relationships, and they were definitely stuck in a past life with that person. We were able to get the memory to come up in the session and get it cleared. If we cannot get the person to look at it in a session, there is always the option of calling one of my clairvoyants. I am willing to give out their number if need be.

What Markus says about Karma

The cause and effect of thought is the main "karma." Thought always precedes results; form is always preceded by an idea of that form. Therefore, it is essential that we clean our minds of the memories of painful and traumatic incidents, so they are not repeated. This is done through a sincere and constant forgiveness practice.

Karma is not some "punishment" for doing "bad things." It is more like a "tendency" or "habit of thinking" that *tends* to give you the same end results. Or it is a playing out of a "pay back" for some guilt you may be feeling. "Guilt demands punishment," we say, but the guilt is something you decide to maintain. So, all "punishment" is self-induced by any guilt you may be hanging onto from the past.

But in the present, there is no guilt. "Forgiveness is the key to happiness," Jesus says in *A Course in Miracles*. He does not make your mistakes into "sins" that cannot be corrected. Rather, He points out that your true Self did not even make the mistakes. Only the ego is capable of making "errors," and these are easily corrected in seeing that you are not your ego. You are a holy Son of God, or Daughter of God, worthy of the grace of the Atonement, which is complete forgiveness. In this state of being, there is no Karma.

36. CLEARING THE DEATH

URGE IN RELATIONSHIPS

The death urge is the secret or suppressed wish to die. It is not a natural urge, but one created in the human mind. It will affect us physically—the body will quite literally self-destruct if this urge is not dealt with directly. In addition, this impulse can affect your personal interaction "killing off" your relationships if you are not careful. The unconscious death urge originated eons ago when we decided we were separate from God. All disharmony stems from this separation. The concept of separateness is also an integral part of the belief system that considers death as inevitable.

The death urge can be an outgrowth of religious, family, and societal programming on death or our experiences with the death of a loved one. It may stem from our anger and rejection of life or a combination of these factors. The urge to die is present in any anti-life thought. It may manifest itself in an obvious way, or it may assume the disguise of religious doctrine, for example, the belief that Heaven is elsewhere—so that death becomes desirable or attractive.

A Course in Miracles sees death as a result of a thought called the ego, just as life springs from a thought called God (Text p 388). God did not create death; we did. And we have nurtured it with lifetimes of accumulated negative thinking. From early childhood we have been told about our soul's potential immortality. There are immortals in the Bible. The idea that our body also has the potential to regenerate itself is never considered, however, even though Jesus says, "The power of life and death are in the tongue." Because we have the ability to live as long as we chose, all death is actually suicide.

Most people slowly kill themselves each day simply by thinking that "death is inevitable." Once established in our minds, this idea is projected onto our relationships with others. Because of this thought, a couple could go through what we call the "death urge of the relationship" sooner or later. We can see this process in action; either one or both of the partners insidiously destroys the relationship—often without even knowing it. I have seen a lot of people "kill off" their relationship soon after a parent died. That is because that family death triggered their own death urge.

Some individuals act out the death urge within their own bodies, creating illnesses. Others sabotage their careers. Some act it out in their relationships, tearing them apart, and others in all three areas, demolishing everything they have. It is not difficult to figure out when our own death urge is surfacing. Everything starts dying on you. Your plants may wither, pets may get sick or die, your appliances break down, your car conks out, your body falls apart and you may also feel depressed, moody or really sick.

Occasionally, none of these symptoms appear because you've suppressed your urge to die. You may be the kind of person who acts your death urge out in one area only—your relationships. In our daily interactions there are a number of ways that we kill off the vitality of our relationships. These can be corrected if you are vigilant.

- ❖ Not being in present time.
- ❖ Not being spiritually awake or spiritually nourished.
- ❖ Buying into prophesies of doom.
- ❖ Failing to express your creativity.
- ❖ Expressing constant negativity, put downs, and disapproval.
- ❖ Failure to forgive.
- ❖ *Stuffing feelings.

❖ Addictions.

❖ Stuffing food, getting fat, smoking.

❖ Control and dependency.

❖ Giving away your power.

❖ Shutting down.

❖ Staying depressed.

❖ Creating a lot of sickness. Etc.

Some relationships that survive the death urge frankly should not. At times, divorce is a positive move. When a partnership has become spiritually bankrupt, it may be time to release it. And obviously if your children are being harmed psychically or physically, you must consider separation. When I see couples that are in doubt, I offer this prayer:

"I pray for this relationship to be healed OR something better for both people."

That way either decision is a win situation. But there are times when a relationship is already dead by the times the couple seeks help, and the partners simply don't have enough desire to resurrect it. But often I see couples who really want to stay together and they are simply coping with the death urge in their relationship. If so, we can help them through it. But it takes a lot of work and breathwork is crucial.

If you and your partner truly want to be together, yet it feels like your relationship is dying, you should consult someone who understands how the unconscious death urge operates. I would recommend you see a breathworker who has already cleared a lot of their own death urge. Ideally, they will understand physical immortality and know that death is not necessary. An immortalist will remind you that out of the great light of God came the spark that was human life. This spark has the same energy and intelligence and power as God. You can recapture that spark and use its Infinite Intelligence to renew your life urge. This cannot be done in just one LRT although that is a good start. We recommend you spend more time with us and come on the spiritual retreats we offer in India, Bali, Glastonbury and Iceland.

In mortal relationships where both partners are convinced that death is inevitable, their union is governed by fear, urgency, mistrust, and constant worry. "When is this person going to die, and leave me?"

When two people know that the choice to keep living is theirs, then unlimited possibilities unfold. But you really have to want immortality to attain it. You have to break the cycle strengthened by anti-life thought patterns. If your life is not working, you will have no desire to live a long time—yet the reason it is not working is that you have not convinced yourself that you really want to live.

37. PHYSICAL IMMORTALITY

I know of nothing that will revitalize a relationship like the goal of physical immortality. (That means the ability to live as long as you chose while improving your body.) We are not talking about living hundreds of years in an old decrepit body. If people are unhappy, they will not be interested in this idea, but on the other hand, if they choose life, then they will be happy! Most people also feel unsettled by the idea of living so long; and the concept might even strike them as "anti-spiritual" since it differs so markedly from traditional church doctrine. Nothing could be farther from the truth. Life is sacred. When you choose more life, you become holier. Such a choice is absolutely spiritual.

I am not the only woman who writes on this subject in case you think this is crazy. Other Immortalists such as Anna Lee Skarin broke ground with this idea and actually learned to dematerialize and rematerialize. Here is a quote from her book, *The Celestial Song of Creation.*

"Death itself begins with the cells and the tissues as they are gradually undermined and destroyed by the vibrations of all negative evil thoughts and fears. Death comes because the individual himself relinquishes the gift of life. He permits the life force to be so crowded out by his own tired, resentful, self-pitying thoughts: his negative attitudes, degenerative desires and greedy actions.

Every discordant negative word and attitude are but destructive forces of death bombarding the life of man. The life principle is gradually crowded out and defeated by mans' ignorance."

So, in others words, the body dies when it can no longer clear itself.

So, this is where Liberation Breathing comes in. You have a way to clear your body. It is a lifelong spiritual path.

The gift of life is exalted and increased through joy, right thinking, and the positive force of right action. Skarin goes on to explain that as the sacred life force increases, old age and physical deterioration ends. They are conquered as the cells of the body are spiritualized and released from death.

This is what the Bible calls "overcoming"—death is conquered through the exaltation of love, praise and gratitude. Vibrations of ecstasy and inner praise nurture the vibration of light. You may choose life over death any time.

What might be blocking you from making this choice? If you knew you could live on and on in your physical body, would you be pleased?

If not, your life probably matches one of the following descriptions:

   a.   You are neither enjoying daily existence, nor winning at the game of life.

   b.   Your daily life is okay or fine, yet you still believe there is a higher place.

If you fall into the first category, you'll ask, "Why would I want to live forever when I am not feeling good now?" A very good question, and yet its answer reveals a paradox. The only way to feel really good is to give up the death urge! (Yes I am repeating this, but most people need to read it many times.)

If you fall into the second category, hear this: Death is not a solution.

You don't necessarily go to a higher place once you have released the body. Check out what the book *Door of Everything* has to say."

"When one choses to die, death does release the weight of gravity and temporarily frees the soul from earth. But it does not change the vibration of consciousness from the

SONDRA RAY & MARKUS RAY

human level. There is no escape from the vibration of yourself except through practiced change of thought. Nor does death cause the released consciousness to go to a celestial level. Consciousness, when departing from the body, automatically seeks its own level. Every lifetime is a new chance to be enlightened and anointed with the light and to rise above the trap of death. For he who has joined to Him that is immortal, will also become immortal."

The fact that one's body may feel perfectly healthy right now does not mean one has "handled" physical immortality. The death urge may very well be suppressed or be acted out in other areas of our life as I have said. The unconscious death urge can be breathed out, but this is a long process. It contains the following:

- ❖ Invalidation of personal divinity (for example with your personal lie).
- ❖ Lack of immortal philosophy
- ❖ Belief systems fostering disease
- ❖ False religious doctrine
- ❖ Family traditions
- ❖ Overeating and other addictions
- ❖ Unresolved tensions and birth trauma
- ❖ Guilt

When you work out all that, you become very vital. You may say, "That is too much. I would rather have fun."

Working this out *is* fun and you will have a lot more fun later. Your other choice is to keep dying and reincarnating and going through it all again. There will be one lifetime when you will finally understand this so why not do it now instead of going through many lifetimes before you accept it?

Some critics say that this idea is the ultimate self–aggrandizement. Quite frankly, if Immortalists were merely striving to live out an endless, purposeless existence, I would agree with them. But this is not the case. The real passion for immortality grows out of a selfless dedication to divine service.

You may wonder why I am spending so much time on this topic in a book on relationships. Precisely this: It all leads to what we call *The Immortal Relationship*.

I found my ideal relationship later in my life. Why would I want to start *checking out* when I just started receiving my deepest spiritual wisdom? And my twin flame? One Immortalist says that "death is a grave mistake." I am writing a new book on this subject called, *Physical Immortality: Live As Long As You Choose, While Improving Your Body*. You can also read my old book on the subject of Physical Immortality: *How To Be Chic, Fabulous, and live Forever!*

38. THE IMMORTAL COUPLE

What is it like to have a relationship between two Immortalists? First of all, let me say that life is totally different. There is a pervasive sense of continual well-being. There is a new feeling of safety and peace. There is less fear because the purpose is to constantly further each other's aliveness. There is plenty of time to handle everything that could come up. The relationship is *eternal*, immediately, and although the couple goes through many changes, *leaving* is no longer an issue. There is an abundance of joy, happiness, and outright bliss. There is a natural telepathy that occurs when the two are apart. Since love is very pure without the projection of the death urge, more spontaneous healing happens in the aura and presence of an Immortalist. Two together provide miraculous energy. They support each other's continuing aliveness always; and this makes it safe to surrender totally. It is like a dream come true.

In the mortalist mentality, there is struggle, illness, pain and the result is death. This sadness of the tragic end to a relationship is overwhelming to the mate left behind. He often feels there is no choice but to die also, and often sees no point in going on "alone." A "deathist" is convinced that there is no way out except to die and he or she has agreed that it is a short life, approximately 70 years. Death is "popular" about 70, and popular ways to kill oneself are to create cancer or heart disease or some similar catastrophe. A *deathist* believes that this is the way it is and that there is no alternative. For this, he often secretly hates God. Two *deathists* will tend to reinforce each other's belief systems and go to the grave together. They have become victims of a belief system handed down through the ages.

An Immortalist knows that this was not the way God intended to call His children home. An Immortalist knows that he can master his body if he masters his thoughts; and that he can continually raise the vibratory rate of his cells to increase his aliveness and youthfulness. He gets together with another Immortalist who helps him do this. Together they form a holy relationship for the purposes of spreading light to the world. An Immortalist gravitates toward another who loves life, has positive thoughts and wonderful energy.

So instead of getting old together and dying, imagine the opposite. What if both of you could become ageless as a couple and live together as long as you wanted—even if it were hundreds of years? Sounds farfetched? Not anymore.

We now have the knowledge to make it happen. An immortal is a soul who has already experienced enough male and female incarnations that the birth/death cycle can now be transcended; this soul can stay here to serve as long as it chooses. Now imagine your perfect mate being the same. What this does for a relationship is simply incredible. When a couple strives for this expression of the Divine, they each become strong and healthy; there is a miraculous and free flow of psychic energy. This energy can be channeled into meaningful self-expression. When a couple expresses together the glory of immortality in their life and society, they function as effective instruments for creative action and realization of higher values in the world. They truly discover what life is at its best; and they are willing and happy to share their blossoming relationship with the world.

39. LIBERATION BREATHING

EXPLAINED

The purpose of Liberation Breathing is to be liberated from suffering.

One can also remember and re-experience one's birth to relive physiologically, psychologically, and spiritually the moment of one's first breath and release the trauma of it. The process begins the transformation of the subconscious impression of birth from one of primal pain to one of pleasure. The effects on life are immediate. Negative energy patterns held in the mind and body start to dissolve. "Youthing" replaces aging and life becomes more fun. It is learning how to fill the physical body with divine energy on a practical daily basis.

The Birth Trauma

At the moment of birth, you formed impressions about the world that you have carried all your life; these impressions control you from a subconscious level. Many of them are negative:

- Life is a struggle.
- The universe is a hostile place.
- The universe is against me.
- I can't get what I need.
- People hurt me.
- There must be something wrong with me.
- Life is painful.
- Love is dangerous.
- I am not wanted.
- I can't get enough love.

Your impressions are negative because your parents and others who cared for you didn't know what you needed when you were born and gave you a lot of things you didn't need: Lights were too bright for your sensitive eyes; sounds were too harsh for your ears, and touches of hands and

170

fabrics were too rough for your delicate skin. Some of you, despite the fact that your spines had been curled up for several months, were jerked upside down by your heels and beaten, which produced excruciating pain. Breathing became associated with pain and your breathing has been too shallow ever since.

But the physical pain is nothing compared to the psychic pain of birth. Nature provided that as a newborn you could receive oxygen through the umbilical cord while learning to breathe in the atmosphere (which was a totally new experience after having been in water), but the custom has been to cut the cord immediately, throwing you into a panic where you felt you were surely going to die at birth.

Another significant psychic pain occurred when you were snatched away from your mother and stuck in a little box in the nursery. Most people never recover from this mishandling of the separation of mother and child. For nine months, you knew nothing but the inside of your mother's womb. It was warm and comfortable until it got too small for you. What you needed was to be shown that the world outside is a far more interesting place, with a lot more possibilities than the womb, and that it could be just as comfortable, safe, and pleasurable as the place you had been. However, since your leaving that place was so traumatic, you have probably spent your entire life trying to get back there, never noticing or experiencing the full extent of the possibilities out here.

Fortunately, changes are now being made in the birth process. Frederic LeBoyer, a French obstetrician, delivered babies in dim light, with few sounds. He placed each child on the mother's stomach, holding him gently, and waiting for the child to learn to breathe on his own. He cut the umbilical cord only after it stopped pulsating, and held the child gently in a tub of warm water to show that there are comfortable and pleasurable experiences available outside the womb. The warm water immersion recreates the feelings of being in the womb. In the tub of water the muscles relax, the baby experiments with movement, a smile may appear. Several doctors in this country have adopted this method, and they say that "LeBoyer babies" are more relaxed, cry little or not at all, and seem to expect love and pleasure from their universe. They are brighter, less afraid, and almost never sick.

At the same time as Dr. LeBoyer was developing his process in France, Leonard Orr in California was discovering a way of helping a person at any age to get in touch with his birth trauma and remove it from consciousness. The process Leonard created (called Rebirthing) is very simple and yet extremely powerful. In the beginning, all sessions were done in a hot tub. The Rebirthee entered the tub with a snorkel and nose plug and floated face down while the Rebirther and the assistant gently held him in place. The water proved a powerful stimulus in triggering the experience of being in the womb and being forced out of it. In fact, as the process evolved, it became clear that going in the water for the first rebirth was so powerful that it was too scary for some people. To avoid overwhelming them, we devised the dry rebirth. We noticed that it is the breathing and relaxing in the presence of a Rebirther that is crucial to the success of the rebirth, and not the water, as he'd thought originally. The process works best when a person is dry-rebirthed until he has a breathing release, and then moves into wet rebirths.

It all occurs when people feel they are in an environment safe enough to re-experience their birth. Being in the presence of a breathworker (someone trained who has already worked out his or her own birth trauma) gives the client the certainty that, "I will come out OK." The message is communicated, telepathically and emotionally, to the subconscious mind of the client. In addition, the breathworker will verbally encourage him by a gentle reminder that he survived his own birth the first time, and can do it again.

The experience varies from person to person. As each discovers his negative conditioning, the breathworker assists in the process of rewriting the script by using affirmations. These are written to contradict specifically the negative decisions the person made at birth. So, we create the view that:

❖ The universe and my body exist for my physical and mental pleasure.

❖ I can get all the love I deserve.

❖ I am glad I was born; I have the right to be here.

❖ I am safe, protected by Infinite Intelligence and Infinite Love.

Needless to say, when a person begins to adopt this view of the world, his life changes drastically. So, for all of you who have ever dreamed of being reborn and starting life all over again, it is now possible.

Any negative thought will inhibit the breath, but the most destructive, inhibiting thoughts are negative ones about the breath itself. Therefore, the negative thoughts you had about life itself while taking your first breath are the most damaging to your breathing mechanism. Reliving your first breath is one of the focal points of rebirthing and is one reason why we originally called this spiritual, mental, and physical experience *re birthing.*

Liberation Breathing/ Rebirthing cuts away human trauma at such a fundamental level that the people who complete it are transformed from working on themselves to playing in the universe. Rather than being serious business, all self-improvement games become recreation and leisure activities, which enlighten.

The Breathing Release

The breathing release is the most important aspect of this process. It is a critical release of all your resistance to life. The breathing release happens when you feel safe enough to re-live the moment of your first breath. It is physiologically, psychologically, and spiritually reliving the moment when you started to breathe for the first time. The breath mechanism is freed and transformed so that, from that moment on, a person knows when his breathing is inhibited and is able to correct it. This experience breaks the power of the birth trauma over the mind and body. A portion of the breathing release probably takes place in all genuine breathwork sessions but usually there will be one session with a very dramatic memory.

Hyperventilation

Hyperventilation is the breathing release in process. Hyperventilation (medically described as breathing so deeply that there is a dramatic loss of carbon dioxide in the blood) is usually treated as a disease. It is actually the cure for sub-ventilation, which is inhibited breathing—commonly called *normal* breathing. Hyperventilation is impossible for a person whose breathing is uninhibited.

It is important to discuss hyperventilation because many people think that it is something to fear and they make the rebirthing experience more difficult than necessary.

What is called "hyperventilation syndrome" is a natural part of breathwork. After working with over ten thousand people, we have evolved a new theory of hyperventilation which is unanimously accepted by medical people who have completed their sessions. The new theory is that hyperventilation is a cure for sub-ventilation. The birth trauma inhibits a person's breathing mechanism, causing shallow breathing. When a person breathes normally, fully and freely for the first time, without fear, it automatically produces some changes in the body. After watching ten thousand people successfully make it through a hyperventilation experience, we have concluded that all the person requires is calmness, safety, and encouragement to complete the process. If the person is encouraged to be patient, to breathe naturally and to relax while experiencing his fears, no harmful effects occur.

The reason we breathe in the upper chest for this breath work (and not in the stomach) is because we are trying to heal the damage to the breath mechanism which occurred when the cord was cut too fast.

We have found that if a person has a voluntary rebirthing experience once a week until completion, it produces a feeling of profound health and well-being. After a person has relived the moment of the first breath, then hyperventilation syndrome no longer occurs. A person can breathe as fast and as hard as is physically possible without undesirable effects. Therefore, our conclusion is that hyperventilation is a natural cure and not an illness.

In our work, we learned that breathing fast was not necessary to induce the hyperventilation syndrome; we observed that relaxing in the presence of the breathworker produces the syndrome regardless of the breathing speed. Increasing the breathing speed, as long as the breathing is relaxed, completely eliminates the elements of the syndrome.

When the energy flows evenly and freely in the body, it heals, balances and grounds the person. The rebirthee feels a profound sense of peace, serenity and physical well-being.

The Energy Release

At some point in rebirthing there is a reconnection to Divine Energy and as a result you may experience vibrating and tingling in your body. It starts in different places in different people, and it is often felt throughout the body. This energy reconnects your body to the universal energy by vibrating out tension which is the manifestation of negative mental mass. Negative mental mass can be permanently dissolved by continuing to breathe in a regular rhythm while your body is vibrating and tingling—experiencing your reconnection to the Divine Energy.

Major points of the energy release include the following:

1. Relaxation causes inner and outer breath to merge and the breath opens.

2. When the breath opens, the merging of the inhale with the exhale brings about the experience of Infinite Being on the physical level.

3. This breathing cycle cleanses the mind and body: there isn't necessarily any tingling or vibrating with this cleansing process.

4. The truth is that this special breathing is dissolving and pumping tension and negative thought from the body, and vibrating is incidental to the cleansing process.

5. After the cleansing, Divine Energy is coming in with every breath. There is no sensation, but the increase in vitality and health is evident in the body and one experiences bliss in the mind.

6. The energy release is dissolving resistance to Divine Energy.

The energy release in the body is so dramatic that many people are afraid of the vibrating sensations and try to stop them. If one does that, they could experience cramping. But this not a problem because when the client keeps breathing, the breath releases the cramping. The cramping is due to resistance of the energy. People who have the ability to let go do not get it. Since the energy is your own life-force, you should not try to stop it. When you try to stop your own energy moving in your own body, it can cause tightness and cramping.

A negative thought stored in your body automatically resists the aliveness of Infinite Being. The presence of the well-trained practitioner automatically lowers the resistance; the Liberation Breathing process can help alleviate your pain. Cooperation is the best thing you can do for yourself. The energy release gives you a new body. You feel connected to your body in a wonderful way—sensually —abundant physical energy and a sense of safety and serenity spreads over you. When the rebirthing experience is complete, this serenity becomes permanent.

Symptoms

We think of Liberation Breathing as the ultimate healing experience because your breath, together with the quality of your thoughts, can heal anything. We have seen symptoms, from migraine headaches to sore ankles, disappear as a result of breathwork. Respiratory illnesses, stomach and back pains have disappeared. Frigidity, hemorrhoids, insomnia, diabetes, epilepsy, cancer, arthritis and all kinds of manifestations have been eliminated. These illnesses seem to be caused or prolonged by the birth trauma. People get stuck in birth trauma symptoms and develop medical belief systems about them. Doctors then become mother-substitutes to support an infancy act. In breathwork, we see people go through physiological changes in ten minutes that other people stay stuck in for years and from which they may die.

On the other hand, Liberation Breathing creates a safe environment in your mind and body for symptoms from the past to act themselves out. These are easy to eliminate. Liberation Breathing is for people who are dedicated to aliveness and who desire to live fully, freely and to be healthy in spirit, mind and body.

Everyone who completes Liberation Breathing receives other general benefits. One of the most important is the ability to receive love and have the direct experience of letting it in. During a session, you are physically able to feel the difference between resisting the love and letting it flow in, and touching is not required to get this experience. As a result, people begin to experience more and more bliss in their daily lives without working at it. As a result, the physical body becomes a more pleasurable place to be. When old aches, pains, and tensions are gone forever, even walking can become orgasmic. Another benefit is the increase in psychic awareness.

Liberation Breathing was born out of the wonderful process called Rebirthing. It is our new expression of conscious, connected breathing that invokes the Divine Mother energy into each session. This new enhancement is a tremendous gift and we are happy to be the ones given this responsibility. What a privilege! We were entrusted with this process, instructed to register the name and oversee the quality of Liberation Breathing Practitioners. The inhale and the exhale are connected in a relaxed rhythm in the upper chest (since we are trying to heal the damage done to the breath mechanism at birth) just as we always did in Rebirthing. So then, the breathing is the same as the rebirthing breath. However, the spiritual dimension of Liberation Breathing is the heart of the matter. We incorporate the Divine Mother 108 names into the session by reciting them to the client at the end of the session. Then we do a fantastic completion by doing a special mantra. This way, I was told is nine times more powerful. We have witnessed the incredible, often miraculous results of this added invocation!

Rebirthing Affirmations

1. I am breathing fully and freely.
2. I survived my birth; therefore, my parents and doctor, and I myself, love life more than death and choose my survival.
3. My physical body is a pleasant and wonderful vehicle for my full and free self-expression.
4. I am glad to be out of the womb so I can express myself fully and freely.
5. I now receive assistance and cooperation from people.

6. I am safe, protected by Infinite Intelligence and Infinite Love; people and things no longer hurt me without my conscious permission.

7. I am no longer afraid of my breath.

8. I have the right and ability to express my hostility about my birth without losing people's love and support.

9. I am now willing to see my birth clearly.

10. Feeling all my emptiness won't destroy me.

11. I forgive myself for the pain I caused myself at birth.

12. Energy and vitality are my birthright.

13. My mother loves and appreciates me.

14. My mother is now glad that I was born.

15. My mother is now happy to get me out of the womb.

16. It was a privilege for my mother to have the honor of bringing me into the world.

17. I am the way, the truth and the life. I came through her body and I am glad to be here. The entire universe is glad that I am here.

18. I no longer feel unwanted. The universe rejoices at my presence in it.

19. The universe is singing in my atoms.

20. My mother, father, family and friends are glad that I was born and that I am alive.

Affirmations for Relationships

1. I love myself; therefore, others love me.
2. I am highly pleasing to myself in the presence of others.
3. I am willing to accept love and stop resisting.
4. It is safe to surrender to love.
5. Love is my safety.
6. I am willing to let myself be supported in love.
7. Love always heals me.
8. I always get what I want and I only want good things for me.
9. I only attract loving, good people.
10. I no longer suppress my feelings. I easily express my feelings to others.
11. I now choose pleasure in my life. Pleasure leads to more pleasure.
12. I love God and I love life; therefore, everyone loves me totally.
13. I now have a success consciousness.
14. I forgive my mother for her ignorant behavior toward me.
15. I forgive my father for his ignorant behavior toward me.
16. I am ready to experience compassion, love, and friendship with my parents, no matter where they are.

17. I no longer attract mates who are my parents. I now attract mates in harmony with my highest spiritual thoughts.

18. I forgive myself completely. I am innocent.

19. I no longer need to fail to get even.

20. I am no longer a helpless infant. I love being grown-up and taking responsibility for my creativity.

21. I am willing to let go of the struggle in relationships and allow myself to have an easy, effortless experience.

22. My body is young and healthy and I am healed.

23. It is safe to indulge in all my favorite pleasures in my relationship.

24. The more I pleasure myself, the closer I am to remembering God.

25. I forgive my family for being confused about sex. I forgive them and myself for suppressing sexual feelings.

26. I am willing now for suppressed incestuous feelings to surface safely and pleasurably.

27. My negative patterns are now dissolving effortlessly.

28. Since what I think about expands, I think only about the good things and breathe out the negative things.

29. I love rebirthing myself with my partner and we remember to do this often.

30. My life urges are stronger than my death urges, and as long as I continue to strengthen my life urges and weaken my death urges, I will go on living in health, happiness, and in great relationships.

31. I am now changing my most negative thought about myself to

32. I am now changing my most negative thought on relationships to _____.

33. My partner and I always have and enjoy ever-increasing love, health, happiness, wealth, wisdom, harmony, full self-expression, sexual bliss, and physical immortality.

34. My past is complete. Everything is resolving itself harmoniously.

35. All my past relationships are now clearing up easily and pleasurably.

36. My partner and I give each other abundant psychic space in which we feel comfortable.

37. I now take responsibility for my feelings of jealousy and do not blame it on my state.

38. The more self-esteem I have, the less jealousy I have.

39. My sex life improves daily.

40. Since people treat me the way I treat myself, I am now treating myself fabulously.
41. I am a beautiful lovable person, and I deserve love.
42. Every day, and in every way, I am more and more able to receive.
43. All of my relationships are now loving, lasting, and harmonious.
44. I am always being nourished in my relationships.
45. My communication is always clear and productive in my relationships.
46. I always treat my partner with the utmost kindness.
47. My partner and I easily surrender to the highest spiritual thought.
48. We now always handle our anger in appropriate ways.
49. We both always tell the truth as fast as we can.
50. Every day we express, verbally and physically, more and more love to each other.
51. Our relationship gets more exciting every day.
52. Every day and in every way, we become closer.
53. Every day our relationship becomes more romantic and immortal.
54. Every day we are feeling more passionate and healthier.
55. I give thanks daily for this partner and I acknowledge myself for creating this relationship.

56. My partner and I serve God together and express the Spirit in high fashion by sharing our life and light with the world.

57. Our relationship is filled with joy and fun and miracle consciousness.

58. Our relationship becomes perfect as we become perfect.

59. I can easily create new relationships whenever I want by the power of my mind.

60. Above all else we want peace and joy.

40. MY FIRST CONTACT WITH BABAJI IN THIS LIFE

Two years after my divorce, my ex-husband called me and wanted me to come back. I thought, "Okay, I should try it one more time." So I sent my things to Florida where he was, and I was actually going to leave the next day. That final night in Arizona, I had a visitor. He was friend of mine, a dentist, and he was sitting on the floor across from me. I was sharing with him how I felt about going back. Suddenly a shocking thing happened. I heard a voice out loud in the air. This voice was not in my head. It was my first *mystical* experience. It was outside my head, and in fact he heard it too, fortunately. Otherwise I would have been more freaked out. The voice said loudly, "NEVER GO BACK!" Then a light entered my body and I could not move. The voice got louder and it said, "NEVER GO BACK. GO TO CALIFORNIA — NOW." My friend looked at me and said, "Sondra, I think you better go to California." What came out of me was this comment: "If I don't follow this voice, I will regret it my whole life."

I could not believe I was saying that however for several reasons:

❖ The California Nurse's association had sent me a letter saying that I should not bother coming to California looking for a job, because the waiting list was two whole years. Furthermore, they said it did not matter if I had a Master's degree.
❖ I did not know one person in California.
❖ I had sent all of my "stuff" to Florida.
❖ I did not have any money, as I had just blown it on a trip to Europe.

The next day I was in my sports car crossing the desert driving to California. I do not remember anything about this trip. I was kind of in a trance. I do remember however, that when I saw the sign for California, and I crossed the line, I started feeling a lot better.

I did not even know where to go — Southern California, or Northern California. I turned the car toward

Northern California suddenly, because I remembered reading about some people in San Francisco who were doing research I was interested in. I thought, "Maybe I can work with them, somehow."

I arrived in San Francisco and I was quite shocked at the steep hills. I went up and down and somehow ended up in the Marina. When I got to the bottom of that hill, my car suddenly went DEAD. I looked up and the street I was on was called Scott Street. That was my name at the time: Sondra Scott. I looked up again and there was a sign on the building that said, "Furnished Apartment for Rent."

"Well," I thought, "I definitely need a furnished apartment." So, I knocked on the door of the manager, and I said to him, "I need to live here." He said, "Ma'am, you need the first month's rent, the last month's rent and the security deposit." He added that up and I definitely *did not* have that money. "I don't have that." I said, "But I need to live here." He said, "Ma'am I told you—you need— etc." We went back and forth, then all of a sudden that same light filled my body and I could not move! I think he was shocked that I was not leaving. Then he suddenly added, "Well, I don't know what it is about you lady, but I will let you move in without any money. I have not done this in 25 years." I thanked him and suddenly blurted out, "I will get a job tomorrow." I could not believe I said that. So then, I got my car going somehow.

The next day I drove to the place where they were doing the research I had read about. They were kind enough, but said they did not have any budget to hire me. "But," one of the people said, "Maybe we can help you get a job." They made one phone call to Kaiser Hospital in Berkeley, and I got hired on the spot. I still don't know how they knew who to call, and how I got a job when the waiting list was two years! The really amazing thing was this: It turned out to be the perfect job to prepare me for my destiny. I was hired as a nurse practitioner in a clinic for pregnant women and family planning. Little did I know then, that I would be doing research on how one's birth trauma affects one's life and relationships. It was a really, really good job—and I was amazed how everything fell into place after I followed the *voice*.

How did all these miracles happen? It had to be Babaji. There is no other possible explanation. He was clearly taking over my life, and I had not even met Him yet.

After I got this miraculous job, my life totally took off in other ways in California. Now I know Babaji was behind it all, because I could never, ever have planned it. I had some serious problems: a) Much of my hair had fallen out after my divorce, and I had a bald spot on the top of my head. 2) I still had a mysterious pain in my body for 13 years, which started when my father died. I could get no help from the medical profession to cure this pain. 3) I started having frequent car damage, as my car was getting banged up a lot, even when I was not in it. My car had to be in the shop frequently. This was a real problem, as I had to drive across the Bay Bridge every day to go to work.

I was in a big quandary with these issues. Fortunately, my hairdresser told me about one of her clients she thought I would like to have as a friend. This friend ended up taking me to one of the very early EST trainings and it was kind of outrageous. One day I was sitting in a seminar, and I was crying, as my car had gotten banged up, yet again. Two guys behind me asked me what my problem was, so I told them what I was crying about. They said, "Don't worry, there is a new guru in town and we will take you to him." I said, "I will try anything." Sunday morning, they drove me out to the Santa Cruz Mountains. There was a man standing on a hill with a flip chart. That seemed so odd to see that outside. He was writing on the flip chart what he had coined as "The Five Biggies." In other words, he explained, "These are the five most negative consciousness factors that keep you from being in bliss." When I saw them listed on the chart, I certainly knew that I had not handled any of them, and I also knew that somewhere in that list was the cause and the answer to my three big problems. He listed "The Five Biggies," which I mentioned earlier in this book:

1. **The Birth Trauma**
2. **Specific Negative Thought Structures**
3. **The Parental Disapproval Syndrome**
4. **The Unconscious Death Urge**

5. Other Life Times

I decided that he must be my new teacher. That day I did not even get clear on his name, however. You might say I was too blown away. Two weeks later I was sitting in an Astrology class and some man in the back put out a question to the group. "Who wants to try this new experiment?" To my shock, my hand went up in the air before I knew what I was volunteering for.

I turned around and it was the same guy! Leonard Orr was his name. Then he said, "Okay you have to drop out for a week and come with me." Now, I had this new job, and certainly did not have any vacation time coming. How was I ever going to get a week off?

I knew, however, that I needed to be there. Why else did my hand go up? Who was behind all this? Who had caused me to *volunteer*? So, off I went to Kaiser Hospital headquarters. I decided to go to the head of the whole hospital instead of just the head of the nursing department. That, alone, was daring. I said to this man something that also surprised me. I told the total truth. I said, "I absolutely need a week off for my spiritual development." I think he was so shocked that to this day he may not know he said, "Yes." How could it be that everything was lining up for me so perfectly? After all, this was unprecedented.

Off I went with Leonard Orr and a few other volunteers. This time we went back to the Santa Cruz Mountains to some former nudist camp, where there was a California hot tub sunken in the ground. The night before the *big experiment* Leonard sat by an open fire and explained to us what the birth trauma was. Then he made us get in sleeping bags and stay in them all night—*and* all the next morning. He explained that this would activate our "no exit terror" we had right before coming out of the womb.

It certainly worked. I was number three in the line. Leonard had us each get in the hot tub with him, with a snorkel in our mouth and nose plug. We were told to roll up in the fetal position and breathe in a circular smooth rhythm, with no pause at the top and no pause at the bottom. All I remember is the water was way too hot, and after breathing for a while I released something major as I let out a yell. People carried me to the grass and placed me under a tree. When I opened my eyes, I saw auras around the leaves of the tree. I had never ever seen auras in my life! After a couple of these sessions, the pain left my body completely—the pain, which I had for 13 years! So, I said to myself, "This is Magic!" I immediately asked Mr. Orr how I could become a *Rebirther* like he was. He answered thusly, "Handle your birth trauma and move in with me." Now then, this was really crazy. But I did it.

And so, it happened. I moved into a big house with Leonard Orr and eight others at 301 Lyons Street, in the Haight-Ashbury section of San Francisco. We had no furniture but we placed a redwood hot tub in the basement for wet rebirthing. In those days, we had not yet discovered dry rebirthing. We thought we needed hot water to activate the memory of the womb and birth. But we had the water too hot and some people went nuts, so we finally turned it down to 103° F. We all changed greatly, and pretty soon we realized as pioneers that we had one of the hottest things *out there*. Rebirthing spread like wildfire, especially after we discovered we could do it dry. I began spreading the word everywhere in San Francisco and soon we got invited to come to other cities—then other countries! People were thrilled with the results everywhere we went.

I organized seminars for Leonard Orr, and they were always packed. I began giving talks about Rebirthing in San Francisco and suddenly I became a seminar leader. I was asked to bring Rebirthing to Hawaii, and this was my first time to lead a public seminar. Eventually, out of this experience, I created the Loving Relationships Training, The LRT®. Then I got invited to speak on so many occasions, and before I knew it, I was *on the road.*

When home in San Francisco I would help in the office with various things. One day a strange letter arrived. It was stamped "India," with no town and no return address. On a strange piece of paper was written, "COME TO INDIA," scrawled in a kind of child's handwriting. No signature. I ran to Leonard and said, "Leonard, we've been called!"

Leonard immediately began putting together a group to go to India. I knew I had to be there. It was the same feeling that came over me when I suddenly raised my hand to become part of the great "experiment." But I had no money. I had just given up my nursing career to become a Rebirther. I called a couple I had met in Hawaii, who had loved the LRT. This doctor and his wife had no children, and had plenty of money, so I asked them if they would sponsor my spiritual quest. Miraculously, they said yes, and I was on my way! It was the only time in my life I borrowed money, and I paid them all back in full later. It was the best investment I ever made in myself. The rest is history—how we actually found Babaji. That amazing story is told, along with

Markus's poems and paintings to Babaji, in our new book: *Babaji, My Miraculous Meetings With A Maha Avatar.* You won't be able to put it down!

41. A TRUE MASTER

When your consciousness is awakened by a true Master, like Babaji, your eyes will discover the beauty of creation. Your ears will hear divine words. You will taste Heavenly food. Your feet will bear you throughout space. Your hands will learn to create in finer, higher worlds of the Soul. A true Master like Babaji gives you victory over your weaknesses, which will give you real power.

Babaji emanates beneficial elements for His group. His sole care is to give you elements of higher nature in harmony with Heaven consciousness. You find nothing but blessings near Babaji. He corrects your mistakes. He encourages you; and under His guidance you end up being like a virtuoso! With Him you cannot fall back into inertia; and you feel continuously moved forward into a new life. He draws you along by his words and by His example.

How can you meditate on Heavenly subjects when you have no high ideal that will lift you above your ordinary life? Babaji may have to be severe on His disciples by showing them certain truths for their progress and advancement. (When you are ill, you think it makes perfect sense to swallow disagreeable remedies.) Most people are afraid to tell you the truth. The Master is not. Babaji has to give several injections and a few operations. When he has done this for me, I got so much benefit that is miraculous. His motive is never to demolish someone, but to help him change to become beautiful and to be saved. What He wants is only the best for you. He wants you to be free, to be rich and loved by all.

Nothing can surpass receiving an initiation and wisdom from Babaji. He will give you love you never found even in your own family. The invisible world sends Masters like Him, and if you don't accept them, then you might get other teachers in the form of illness, misery, or difficulties. (If you have to go through these things, then there is probably a karmic reason for it.) Babaji lightens your karma. Babaji is here to help you to *real* freedom—so that you are strong despite all difficulties. He will warn you about what awaits you if you continue on your present path. He can open doors for you, but it is up to you to walk through them. He is an essential tuning fork. You must tune yourself to Him. Then you end up vibrating quite differently.

You must always love and serve a higher being than yourself so that you can perform miracles (thanks to Him) and do well. There is osmosis that goes on between you and Babaji. You benefit greatly from His light. Do you have fear of sacrificing your lower nature? Every moment you can choose a new life! Babaji says, "My love is available, you can take it or not. I say "Why not?" We need all the help we can get, don't we? So why not consider coming with us to India and going to his ashram? We go every spring to Herakhan on the India Quest, to Babaji's home, around March or April. Why don't you join us?

Recently in a meditation I "saw" myself coming toward Babaji for several lifetimes. It was a very winding, curvy, difficult road. At the end of the experience I saw myself on a straight road going directly to Him. How long this has taken, only He knows. But it was exhilarating. A false master is just a tranquilizer. You come to him and he consoles you. But the *real Master* like Babaji will help you grow rapidly. Growth can be difficult—you have to pass through many tests. A true Master will haunt you— there is no transformation without fire. Friction is the right word for the inner war. You have to become uprooted so your family no longer has power over your mind. All that has been before must be disrupted.

Unless you are ready to encounter yourself, you cannot become a true disciple, because a Master can do nothing if you are not ready to face yourself. All that you have denied and repressed will come up—and that gives one fear. That is why people avoid going to Babaji. They are not willing to go through fear. (But, we have breathwork to release this fear, and we do Liberation Breathing every single day on the India Quest in Herakhan.) You only become a disciple when you are ready to expose your whole being to yourself. I always felt totally exposed around Babaji; but He was the most exciting thing on earth! Are you ready? Are you courageous enough? I am daring you to be great! This photo Markus took of me in 1989 at the door of Babaji's personal rooms in Herakahn, His *kutir*.

The Master is like a midwife. He helps you pass through a new birth and be reborn. But you have to trust—you cannot doubt. You have to drop your armor completely. The openness has to be total, otherwise nothing can happen. You have to pass through great training. To me, it is the greatest training on earth.

The Master is the one who awakens you. He wants to birth you into His or Her dimension. But when there is a Master like Babaji, or Ammachi, or Jesus, people try to escape from Him or Her in every way possible. I see this all the time. People say they want to go to Babaji with me and then they back out! People think it is dangerous to encounter Him because He can see right through you and the false life you made up. You become transparent and cannot hide yourself. I used to become a trembling leaf before Babaji. I had to be very courageous around Him. But I took the jump into the Abyss and I gained everything. I want that for you.

Babaji is saying to you: *"The door is open right now. My love is available. You can take it or not."* I say, "Why not, we need all the help we can get!" If you postpone the entry your mind will remain the same. People have tried every which way to change themselves—but is there really much change? The Master is freedom. The Master is fire and you have to become like molten liquid so all that is impure is burned away. At times I felt like my bones were on fire for days and weeks on end. But I knew that this fire purification was what I needed.

I came out different from what I was. A transformation is discontinuity with the past. It is not patchwork. How do you think I ended up with such a great relationship? If you are courageous enough to pass through the fire of Babaji, a new world will open up for you. The other choice is to remain in the nightmare. But one has to decide. The mind is afraid of the unknown. But the unknown is ecstasy. Would I kid you? Babaji and I invite you once again. Are you going to reject the invitation?

Love, Sondra

Babaji and I in Herakhan

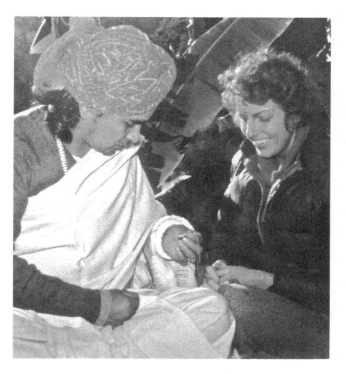

42. THE DECISION FOR

HEAVEN

This is a dialogue Markus and I made in Colorado Springs, CO, USA, for this chapter: The Decision for Heaven. 28—SEPT—2016

SONDRA:

Here we are in Colorado Springs where we are completing *The New LOVING RELATIONSHIPS Book*, which we have totally redone and made new. And we are so excited. To do this one chapter about peace is really important. And, what is the exact line in *A Course in Miracles*, Markus.

MARKUS:

Well, there are a couple of lessons that apply to peace. One is Lesson 185, "I want the peace of God." Then the next lesson that we decided to discuss was, "Heaven is the decision I must make," which is Lesson 138.

SONDRA:

Yes, OK. So, what I've often noticed, after working with hundreds and hundreds of clients, is that most people are addicted to conflict. The ego is addicted to conflict. And, peace is unfamiliar. In fact, peace is uncomfortable for people, because *A Course in Miracles* says that the first obstacle to peace is the "desire to get rid of it." Which means when there is peace, it is so scary, you have to make up an argument to feel more comfortable; which is really too bad, because peace is the thing we want. A lot of people not only are not familiar with peace, they think peace is boring. I guess they like the drama and they think the drama is exciting. But, I know when I have been really in peace I have more joy, and therefore I have had more fun. So, what I want to do is inspire people to choose peace, and for them to know that peace is joy, and peace fun. And I think if people can get that, they will be more inspired to choose peace. Right?

MARKUS:
Well, conflict is very stimulating, in some ways. You know, we go to movies that are very violent; we go to relationships in which we have differences and arguments; and somehow, we feel more alive when we are in this state of conflict.

SONDRA:
Well, That's really too bad, isn't it?

MARKUS:
But isn't that the status quo?

SONDRA:
I guess so.

MARKUS:
We dwell on what doesn't work, rather than focusing on what does work. We dwell on what we don't want, rather than focusing on receiving what we do want.

SONDRA:
But, that's kind of tragic!

MARKUS:

Well it is, but it's the status quo of the human condition. So, on the cutting edge of our human evolution, in this age, we have to see that thought produces result, and therefore we can decide for the thoughts or the feelings that put us in a state of happiness or joy, or peace, and that is a decision we make. We must make it.

SONDRA:

Okay, well, if one makes the decision, does that mean that they can be in peace forever, or does that mean they could slide back and they have to redo the decision?

MARKUS:

Well, let's just say, if you were practicing to become a virtuoso violinist, you were fairly good all ready, and you were maybe even a prodigy, someone like Isaac Stern or Itzhak Perlman, there would be some places in your practice where you would notice you made a mistake. You weren't in a state of perfection in playing, in acting, in producing your highest abilities, perfect music. But you wouldn't allow that mistake to throw you off. You would just say, "Oh, I learned about this mistake in my practice. SO, I'm going to be determined to overcome it and make myself more in a state of perfection, more in a state of Heaven, in a state of perfect music.

SONDRA:
Does that mean okay that we decide for peace, and that we might fall down and not have it, and we have to re-decide. Is that what you are saying?

MARKUS:
No, you make the decision for peace, and that is something you do once with God. You say, "God, above all else I want peace. I am deciding this with You, and You are going to help me undo everything in my life that is not peace."

SONDRA:
Oh, OK. Alright. So that means that we have to be really serious about this, and, we have to give up our addiction to anger. And I think most people are kind of addicted to anger, and they don't know how to get out of it because they have never forgiven. I think the whole lesson would be—you have to forgive everybody 100%. And, you know, we keep asking people, "What is you forgiveness level on your mother, or your father or your sister and so on, and your X." And, zero is no forgiveness and ten is

complete forgiveness. We ask people to pick a number on each person, and they get very low scores. They get five, or four, and say, "Oh, I am moving up to eight today." But, that still isn't good enough, because *A Course in Miracles* says until you have forgiven totally, which would be 100%, you have not forgiven at all. So, a score of eight, or nine, is not good enough. And the problem is, if you are only at nine that means there is one point where it could leak. And what you have not forgiven you attract. So that one point is kind of dangerous. You could attract the same thing that you were angry at. So, I guess, to me, you cannot discuss this topic without discussing forgiveness. Right?

MARKUS:
You can't discuss it without discussing forgiveness. Well, what is forgiveness, then? We have to ask that question. Forgiveness is a state of mind in which you have no grievances toward anyone. Lesson #68 says, "Love holds no grievances." NO grievances; that's like NONE; zero grievances.

SONDRA:
Right.

MARKUS:

So, Heaven is a decision I must make in which I have relinquished all my grievances. I have no judgments toward anyone or anything. And, if I feel an activation, a kind of a difference of opinion with someone, I immediately decide not to go there, not to debate the difference. It's part of conflict, which is part of the ego, of the meaningless world, which is part of *non-Heaven*. So, Heaven is a state in which there is no conflict, there is no grievance. And I have let go of any judgment, any thought that is not in a state of perfect happiness.

SONDRA:
I think we all agree, that if we want total peace, total Heaven, we have to forgive everyone. But why is it so hard for people to forgive?

MARKUS:
Because they want to be *right*.

SONDRA:
They want to be right? Well, why is it so hard for them to "get off" wanting to be *right?*

MARKUS:
Well, because we are addicted to conflict.

SONDRA:

Hmmm.

MARKUS:

You know, there is a place in the Text of *A Course in Miracles,* called *The Rules For Decision.* And it says in that section, when you begin your day you *decide* for peace, for happiness, for joy. And this is a decision you make. You consciously say, "Lord, give me this day, which is Your day, and the nature of this day, which is the nature of all the cosmos, is peace, is happiness, is JOY." So we could all see the wisdom of that decision. Couldn't we?

SONDRA:

Yes. It makes sense to me. But, I am not sure everybody is willing.

MARKUS:

OK. So then, the next thing it says in that lesson, *The Rules For Decision,* is something like this: it says if you are NOT having a happy day, you have to *admit* that *you are wrong.*

SONDRA:

OK.

MARKUS:
So, this is a very important point in making a
decision, because these are called the *Rules For
Decision*. If you are *not* in a state of peace, if you are
not in a state of Joy, if you are not in a state of
absolute perfect happiness, you have to admit *you* are
wrong.
SONDRA:
Oh, OK.

MARKUS:
You are the one causing your own upset. *You* are the
one causing your own hell. If it is not Heaven, it is
hell. If it is not happiness, it is sorrow, irritation,
anger, you name it; discontent, frustration. You can
give any number of names to that state of being that
is not in Heaven; that is not in peace. So, that is your
responsibility, and you have put yourself there.

SONDRA:
That reminds me of the definition of a humble
person: "A humble person recognizes his errors,
admits them, and does something about them." I
think that is really important to emphasize. So, most
people aren't even recognizing their errors. And, if
they do have them they're not even admitting them.
And if they are admitting them, they are not doing

anything about them. So, I think that's a really important thing to mention here. "A humble person recognizes his errors, admits them, and does something about them."

MARKUS:

Well, what is the "does something about them" part? It's like, once you have seen the errors, once you have admitted them, what is that action of doing something about them? And that is what *A Course in Miracles* calls a decision.

SONDRA:

OK.

MARKUS:

You make a decision with God.

SONDRA:

That's the important thing. You make this decision with God, right?

MARKUS:

OK, that involves forgiving yourself for the mistake. But, in order to truly forgive yourself, you have to forgive everybody else for making the same darn mistake.

SONDRA:

Hmmm.

MARKUS:

So, forgiveness is something complete; it is something whole; it is something unequivocal. You can't forgive some people and not forgive other people. You can't forgive you brother, and not forgive *Hitler.*

SONDRA:

Oh!

MARKUS:

You can't forgive your sister, and not forgive other personages from history who have done dastardly deeds—even in your own life. If you are holding grievances towards your next-door neighbor, or your sister, or your mother or your father, you have not totally forgiven— therefore you have not made the decision for Heaven.

SONDRA:

Well, let's say I forgive everybody in my mind, and I think I have, and therefore I decide I want total peace, and that's fantastic. But then I go home and visit my mother, and feel frustrated with her, and I go down from ten to eight, and I see I am upset with her again. So, what happens if you slip back like that?

MARKUS:
It shows you that you are affected by the misperception of separation.

SONDRA:
So, does that mean I have not really forgiven, then, if I slipped back? I have not really made the decision.

MARKUS:
Somewhat.

SONDRA:
Hmmm. That's the problem.

MARKUS:
That is the problem, and that is the challenge. It takes determination to make a decision. Jesus says, "I am *determined* to see things differently." So, if somebody comes to you and they are in a state of duress, or they are in a state of judging you, or they are in a state of attacking you, it takes determination not to make that real, and see them in their true Self, in their Christ Self, in their holy Self. Because if you judge them, if you push them away, if you deter from that union

with them, you are saying, "They are in hell, but I am going to be in Heaven." No, that's not how it works. You have to enter the door of Heaven with everybody else along with you.

SONDRA:
But what if they are not ready to go?

MARKUS:
Well, it does not matter. If they are under the illusion of sorrow, of separation, of bla bla bla, whatever you want to call it, that's meaningless thought. Now, they may not feel the Heaven that you are deciding for, but they are also the beneficiaries of your decision for Heaven.

SONDRA:
Ok. Well, that's really good. But what about people who think peace is boring? They like the drama, and drama is exciting, and they think that peace is boring and peace is no fun.

MARKUS:
Well, the body likes to be stimulated, the body likes drama, the body likes all kinds of activations, physical goodies; that's the very thing you need to forgive. So, it doesn't mean that those things are

inherently wrong. It is what Esther Hicks would call *contrast* —the contrast between what you want and what you don't want. So often we want that which is harmful, that which in the moment seems like it is very stimulating and gratifying, but in the end, it sort of dashes us into the doldrums.

SONDRA:
Right. Well you know for me, I have discovered that peace is wonderful, and peace is Joyful. And when you are in Joy, you really do have fun. So, I have discovered that, you know, peace is fun. And most people do not have that thought, but I'd like to share that with people. That's my experience.

MARKUS:
Well, Heaven is not boring. When you are doing something that's creative, truly creative, that means it's Joyful. That means that you are extending something to the whole of creation, to all your brothers and sisters. And that's very inspiring. It's inspiring to you, and inspiring to those who receive the gift of whatever it is you are extending. So, if you an artist, or a writer, or you are even an accountant and you love the order of numbers, that which you are extending to your fellow men, your fellow sisters and brothers, is something of your God-given talent.

And that is very uplifting, that's Joyful. That's in a state of Heaven. So, we have to make the physical extension of whatever it is we are offering *in* this state of peace—that's certainly not boring. That's dynamic, that's creative.

SONDRA:

You know, I was studying the lesson, "I could see peace, instead of this," for one year. (Lesson #34 in ACIM) And at the time I was involved with this man, and he was rich. So, I was kind of dazzled because I had never dated a rich man. I moved in with him before I really looked at the problems I was going to face with him. So, I moved in and this relationship only lasted one day. It was kind of funny. Anyway, I was unpacking my bags, and I was having a good time as usual, and he started picking a fight with me. And I said, "Hey, I am not going to go there with you. I deserve peace in my personal life." And he got really angry and he stormed out of the apartment. And I thought, "Wow, this relationship is not going to work. This relationship didn't last very long." So, I started packing my bags. And I thought, "What will my mother think? What will my friends think if I end this relationship in one day?" And then I thought, "No, I really want to pass this test. I want to choose peace."

Anyway, he came back in the apartment, and he said, "OK, I thought it over, and you're right. You deserve peace. But, I can't live like that." He actually said that. And I said, "I can see that. That's why I am packing my bags." And it was amazing. He even admitted he couldn't live in peace. And it was such a huge lesson for me. And I was so happy that I passed the test, and I chose peace instead of going on with this relationship. Because, it was very tempting to think, "O well, I can change him, etc., etc." But my higher self knew that was not going to be possible. So, that was an interesting experience I had on one of these *Course in Miracles* lessons.

MARKUS:

I would say that was a demonstration of a *decision* that you made. And therefore, it was a true miracle. It was a shift in your perception that said, "I can see *peace* instead of *this*." And that is the miracle that you experienced, that you witnessed. And in seeing that peace, and in also hearing his denial in himself of accepting that peace, you said, "Well, this relationship is over," and you moved on. So, how many people would be that swift in their decision? No, they would say, "Well, I am attached to the money; I am attached to the environment; I am attached to this choice that I made; I can't disappoint my mother; I can't disappoint my family." And they would have stayed in that relationship, which would have continued to be in a state of conflict. So, in that very instant was a miracle — when you said, "I can see that. You've decided that you *don't* want peace. But my decision *is* for peace, and therefore, we have nothing to relate to."

SONDRA:

Right, and it was because I was reading *A Course in Miracles* that I was able to do that. If I hadn't been studying *A Course in Miracles,* I would have gotten stuck there, and it would not have worked out. So, I am very grateful to the *Course* for teaching this whole lesson on peace. And, I think it's something everybody should study if they want to get through this block.

MARKUS:

Absolutely. My teacher, Tara Singh, said, "*A Course in Miracles* is the greatest gift America has given to mankind, in this time, " — bar none. So, are we going to wake up and listen to it; and decide for Heaven, and decide for miracles, and change our mind, and replace our thought system of conflict with our inherent spiritual thought system of peace and Joy and Love?   Or are we going to go on with our baloney? So, we have the means to make a decision for peace, and *A Course in Miracles* is the *roadmap* for that.

SONDRA:
Thank You.

MARKUS:
God bless you.

WORKS CITED

- ❖ Mata Amritanandamayi—The "Mother" from the book *Awaken Children*
- ❖ Dick Sutphen—*We Were Born Again to Be Together*
- ❖ Dr. Roger Woolger—*Other Lives, Other Selves*
- ❖ Foundation for Inner Peace—*A Course in Miracles*
- ❖ May McCarthy—*The Path to Wealth*
- ❖ Tara Singh—*How to Raise a Child of God*
- ❖ Fredric LeBoyer—*Birth Without Violence*
- ❖ Dr. Michel Odent—*Birth Reborn*
- ❖ Dr. Thomas Verney—*The Secret Life of the Unborn Child*
- ❖ Leonard Orr—*Breaking the Death Habit*

RESOURCES

SONDRA RAY:

Website: www.sondraray.com
Blog: www.liberationbreathing.blogspot.com
Facebook Profile: www.facebook.com/sondra.ray.90
Facebook Page: www.facebook.com/LiberationBreathing
Instagram: www.instagram.com/SondraRay
Twitter: https://twitter.com/sondraray1008
E-mail: immortalrayproductions@gmail.com
Amazon Author Page:
http://www.amazon.com/author/sondraray

MARKUS RAY:

Website: www.markusray.com
Blog: www.markusray.wordpress.com
Facebook Profile: www.facebook.com/markus.ray.169
Facebook Page: www.facebook.com/LiberationBreathing
Facebook Page: www.facebook.com/markusray.artist
Twitter: https://twitter.com/MarkusRay1008
Instagram: https://instagram.com/markusray1008/
Pinterest: www.pinterest.com/markusray/
E-mail: markus.ray@aol.com
Amazon Author Page:
http://www.amazon.com/author/markusray

REQUEST TO OUR READERS

It has been our joy to share this material with you, our readers. Life has brought us together, and we hope to hear from you about the "miracle manifestations" in your relationships as a result of reading this book.

Also, we welcome you to write a review on Amazon for this book, and also other Sondra Ray and Markus Ray books you have read.

We hope to see you on one of our Seminars or Quests around the world. We invite you to have a Liberation Breathing session with us. Go to www.SondraRay.com to register for Seminars and Quests and/or to book a Liberation Breathing session.

ABOUT THE AUTHORS

Sondra Ray is known the world over as one of the most dynamic spiritual leaders of our day. She is recognized by many as a spiritual teacher, author, lecturer, and healer, with a renowned expertise in the area of relationships, sacred lifestyles, Sacred Quests, and Rebirthing/Breathwork she now calls Liberation Breathing®.Sondra graduated with a degree in nursing from the University of Florida in the early 1960's. Inspired by President Kennedy's inauguration speech, she was a pioneer in the first 10 groups of the Peace Corps, an experience that gave her the lifelong dedication to world service. After the Peace Corps, she served her country as a US Air Force nurse, during the Vietnam era, counseling the families of pilots killed in action. *

In the early 1970's Sondra Ray teamed with Leonard Orr who together explored the effects of the "birth trauma" and its detrimental subconscious influence on a person's life. They discovered the powerful use of conscious connected breathing (Rebirthing) to be an effective practice to help people clear these memories of early life trauma very quickly from their mind and body. Sondra went on to write over 20 books on the subjects of Rebirthing, Liberation Breathing®, relationships, ideal birth, The Forgiveness Diet©, A Course in Miracles, healing and holiness, and the many mental & spiritual imperatives in life.

Author Marianne Williamson says of Sondra Ray:

"...those who explored the frontiers of universal spiritual consciousness were true pioneers. Their ideas were mind blowing and life altering for an entire generation, for whom such beliefs were startlingly outside the box. One of those pioneers was Sondra Ray...If Sondra writes a new book, I read it. I let go of my left brain and drink her in, imagining her sitting on a chair, explaining to me what to her is so obvious and the rest of us, well, maybe not so much. I have never experienced Sondra as anything other than a beam of light—I have lived enough to be able to say that of all the good fortunes I have had in my life, encountering her has been one of the liveliest. Sondra Ray is more than a woman — The word goddess comes to mind..."

From Marianne Williamson's Foreword in Sondra's book, *Rock Your World with the Divine Mother.*

Ray was launched into international acclaim in the 1970s as one of the pioneers of the Rebirthing Experience. She has trained thousands of people all over the world in this conscious connected breathing process, and is considered one of the foremost experts on how the birth trauma affects

one's body, relationships, career and life. As she puts it, "This dynamic breathing process produces extraordinary healing results in all of your relationships with your mate, with yourself and with Life—very fast. By taking in more Life Force through the breath, limiting thoughts and memories, which are the cause of all problems and disease, come to the surface of the mind so they can be 'breathed out', forgiven and released."

Now Sondra Ray has taken Rebirthing to a new level of effectiveness by invoking the Divine Mother energy into the breathing sessions. One of her recent books, *Rock Your World with the Divine Mother*, emphasizes the importance of a fundamental paradigm shift out of the conventional "patriarchal model" of relationships into a more balanced equality between the Masculine and Feminine polarities. This has also been an influence on her teachings in the Breathwork field. In her most recent book on this subject, *Liberation Breathing®: The Divine Mother's Gift*, she describes a new expression of Rebirthing in which attention is paid to the underlying Life Force of matter, referred to as the Divine Mother Energy. This Energy has great healing potential as invoked in the Liberation Breathing® process.

Often ordained as the "Mother of Rebirthing and Breathwork", Sondra created and teaches various seminars, including her most popular Loving Relationships Training®, which has evolved into the New LRT®, which will soon be offered as an online interactive course. This training has helped thousands of people get clear on their relationships. It explains common negative family patterns and helps people overcome them through applying practices of Liberation Breathing® and affirmations of creative thought. Ray has taken these seminars and practices across the globe to countries such as England, France, Spain, Italy, Germany, Iceland, Ireland, Poland, Sweden, Estonia, Russia, South America, New Zealand, Australia, Singapore, Bali and Japan. She also takes groups to India, Glastonbury, Iceland, Bali and Hawaii for annual pilgrimages. See here for Sondra Ray and Markus Ray's worldwide schedule:

https://www.sondraray.com/events

Sondra Ray also had the privilege of spending time in India with the immortal Master, Maha Avatar Haidakhan Babaji on several occasions from 1977-1984, becoming His lifelong student and disciple. The inspiration for this book, He is the immortal "Yogi-Christ" spoken about in Yogananda's *Autobiography of a Yogi*, Chapters 33 & 34. For the past 30 years Sondra has led groups to India to Babaji's ashram in the Himalayas, and introduced thousands to the deep spiritual heritage this country has to offer. Her India Quest is given every Spring, on which she takes people to the Banks of the Ganges, to Haidakhan, to participate in the Spring Navaratri, a nine-day spiritual festival dedicated to honoring the Divine Mother—the feminine aspects of the Divine Nature that permeates all Life. Participants are also immersed in the Liberation Breathing® process daily during the India Quest, her most powerful offering of the year.

Ms. Ray currently travels the world teaching, and has a private healing practice with her husband, Markus Ray. They conduct private Liberation Breathing® sessions in person and over Skype. People who have worked with Sondra Ray & Markus Ray say their teachings, their guidance, their dynamic presence, and the Liberation Breathing® process have saved them years of time in getting clear on relationships and deeper connection and communication with a mate.

Sondra was one of the first to lecture on and teach *A Course in Miracles,* since the late 1970's. She has said, "*A Course in Miracles* is the most important book written in 2000 years." Together with her husband, Markus, who studied *ACIM* with pre-eminent teacher, Tara Singh,** for 17 years, they travel the world speaking on this profound scripture. Tara Singh has described *A Course in Miracles* as "A Gift for All Mankind," destined to be one of the greatest gifts America has contributed to the world of spiritual literature. Sondra & Markus will be offering a one-year online study program for *A Course in Miracles*, "Miracles for You," in 2017, in which their knowledge and support for serious students can be shared.

Applying over 40 years of metaphysical study, Ray has helped thousands of people discover how their negative thought structures, birth trauma, habitual family patterns and unconscious death urge have affected their life. She encourages people to make lasting positive changes through Liberation Breathing® to be more free, happy and productive. No matter what Sondra Ray is doing, she is always trying to bring about a higher consciousness. Recently she has written *Spiritual Intimacy: What You Really Want With a Mate.* This is a guidebook for finding, creating and maintaining a holy relationship with your mate in the new paradigm of a conflict-free lifestyle. And the latest book on her master: *Babaji: My Miraculous Meetings With A Maha Avatar.*

Markus Ray received his training in the arts, holding an MFA in painting from Tyler School of Art, Temple University in Philadelphia, PA, USA. Also, a writer and a poet, he brings spirituality and sensuality together in these mediums of expression. He is the author of a major work, *Odes To The Divine Mother,* which contains 365 prose poems in praise of the Divine Feminine Energy. Along with the *Odes* are his paintings and images of the Divine Mother created around the world in his mission with Sondra Ray. This work is available on Amazon and in bookstores.

Markus is a presenter of the profound modern psychological/spiritual scripture, *A Course In Miracles*. He studied *ACIM* with his master, Tara Singh, for 17 years, in order to experience its truth directly. In his last book, *Miracles My Master, Tara Singh: Applications of A Course in Miracles,* he gives account of his years with Mr. Singh and the experiences he received from this holy relationship. It is also available on Amazon.

Markus Ray's spiritual quest has taken him to India many times with Tara Singh and Sondra Ray, where Muniraj, Babaji's foremost disciple, gave him the name Man Mohan, "The poet who steals the hearts of the people". In all of his paintings, writings and lectures, Markus creates a quiet atmosphere of peace and clarity that is an invitation to go deeper into the realms of inner stillness, silence and beauty. He teaches, writes and paints along-side of Sondra Ray, and many have been touched by their demonstration of a holy relationship in action. His iconic paintings of the Masters can be viewed on www.MarkusRay.com which he often creates while his twin flame, Sondra Ray, is lecturing in seminars.

Babaji, Jesus and the Divine Mother painted by Markus

Sondra Ray & Markus Ray are brought together by the grace of their Master, Maha Avatar Herakahn Babaji. Babaji Himself said, "Markus is my humbleness. Sondra is my voice. Together they are my Love." As ambassadors for Him, their mission is to bring His teaching of "Truth, Simplicity, Love and Service to Mankind" along with the presence of the Divine Mother to the world. They do so through seminars like the New LRT®, the healing practice of Liberation Breathing®, and the study of A Course in Miracles. They are unfolding the plan of Babaji, Jesus and the Divine Mother, whom they refer to as the "dream team."

Their relationship is a shining example of what is possible through deep ease and no conflict. They can take you to a higher realm where spiritual intimacy, miracles, and holy relationships can become real in your life. Their various Sacred Quests around the world with Liberation Breathing®

prepare many to heal their relationships, to receive more profound levels of divine presence in their lives, and awaken more awareness of immortal Love in their hearts. Markus writes this early poem of his relationship with Sondra:

My Immortal Love for You

My Immortal Love for You is beyond the stars.

My Immortal Love for You is never ceasing, but strong from the heart of the Master within us.

My Immortal Love for You is in the quiet of the night which envelops our sleep in sweetness.

My Immortal Love for You fuels my desire to place myself within the inner spaces of your receptive pull.

My Immortal Love for You rests in the cozy safety of refuge amidst all thunderous storms.

My Immortal Love for You makes all its beautiful sounds of music in the cadence of daily speech.

My Immortal Love for You provides all that we need in this world.

My Immortal Love for You has no fear, no matter what our situation may look like.

My Immortal Love for You cannot be extinguished in any way.

My Immortal Love for You is a beacon of light when all other lights have gone out.

My Immortal Love for You is the reason I am here now.

My Immortal Love for You is the source of all my songs.

My Immortal Love for You pervades the molecules of all things seen and unseen.

My Immortal Love for You lifts other souls to the heights of their own immortal being.

My Immortal Love for You is the spark of my internal fires.

My Immortal Love for You warms my whole body in the cold caverns of temporary doubt.

My Immortal Love for You is the first thought in my day and the last thought before my sleep.

My Immortal love for You is the medicine for all my sickness, the balm that heals all of my wounds.

My Immortal Love for You is the well of infinite waters into which your ladle dips to quench your thirst.

My Immortal Love for You is the new beginning that holds out its infinite promise of perfect happiness.

So, would I immerse myself in You, the spring that feeds forever this awareness of my Immortal Love for You.

Sondra Ray and Markus Ray on their wedding day in India

*In her early formative years before her life mission as a Rebirther, teacher and author, Ray earned a B.S. degree in Nursing from the University of Florida College of Nursing, and a Master's Degree in Public Health and Family Sociology from the University of Arizona. She was trained as a Nurse Practitioner in Obstetrics and Gynecology. During her assignment in the Peace Corps she was stationed in Peru, which prepared her for world service. During her service in the US Air Force she was stationed at Luke Air Force Base in Arizona.

**Tara Singh, author, humanitarian, lecturer on *A Course in Miracles* was trained by Mr. J. Krishnamurti for over 30 years to prepare him for 3 years in silence—out of which came the blessing of his meeting with Dr. Helen Schucman, the scribe of *A Course in Miracles*. It was his intense relationship with Dr. Schucman, on a daily basis for over 2 and 1/2 years, that served to ordain Tara Singh as one of the most authentic voices on this modern-day scripture available in these times.

AFTERWORD

Your Most Important Loving Relationship

Thank you for reading this book on Loving Relationships by Sondra Ray. As her husband, Markus Ray, I can honestly say we have a truly loving relationship because we put our spiritual life in the first place. We do various daily spiritual practices together, as described in our book, *Spiritual Intimacy*; we travel around the world and teach together; we are each other's confidant; we process each other when we are having a negative experience; and we have "more fun per hour." Sondra is my teacher, my lover, my *ascension buddy* and my best friend. There is a song by the folk-singer, John Prine, that describes a kind of humorous relationship we often laugh about: *She Is My Everything*.

However, kept in perspective, we are both clear that our most important relationship is with our own Divine Source. There is a lesson in *A Course in Miracles* that says:

"There is no Love but God's" Lesson 127

That is a pretty strong statement. Are we even aware of its unequivocal meaning? Loving relationships that we have known, which we all say we want more of, with more connection, more joy, more communication, more understanding, more sex, more money, more happiness, more satisfaction, have often left out the *God factor*. What is God's Love, which the lesson says in the *only* Love?

Well, defining Love is like defining God. What good would it do to say some meaningless thing about it? Both are beyond description. But the *Course* also states in the introduction to the Text:

> *The course does not aim at teaching the meaning of love, for that is beyond what can be taught. It does aim, however, at removing the blocks to the awareness of love's presence, which is your natural inheritance.*

So, there is no Love but God's, and the action of miracles is to "remove the blocks" to our awareness of Love's presence. We all find ourselves in a worldly life of practical things—of schools, of jobs, of family responsibilities, of relationships with friends and colleagues, of career demands, of transportation here and there, etc. But we also have a sense for something sacred, a yearning for something higher and more fulfilling than the lives and routines we have made. A lot of friction in our everyday lives arises. What do we do about it? Love and conflict cannot occupy the same space in the mind.

What is your most important Loving relationship? You may think it is with your mate, but what is the Energy behind this relationship which makes it "loving?" Is the energy of your relationship with your mate Harmonious? Fulfilling? Joyful? Self-sustaining? New? Inspiring? Happy? Peaceful? Or is it stuck in the common patterns of anger, resentment, living under the same roof in a kind of polite hell of convenience?

Many marriages and partnerships break up, to the tune of 50% of the time in the USA. We have grown accustomed to relationships that do not last. They have, it seems, a "shelf life," a predetermined "expiration date." The old paradigms are not working, but the new paradigms seem fleeting and loosely committed. Is there permanence in Love? Can you count on it to prevail in all situations? Is there an Absolute Love that is unaffected by time and the energy of conflict? What is the Energy we need to tap into to have this Love of the Absolute in our lives? Do we even want that?

God's Love is an Energy. This Energy has created and is creating the universe. This Energy is described very well in Lesson 127:

Love is one. It has no separate parts and no degrees; no kinds nor levels, no divergences and no distinctions. It is like itself, unchanged throughout. It never alters with a person or a circumstance. It is the Heart of God, and —Love's meaning is obscure to anyone who thinks that love can change. He does not see that changing love must be impossible. And thus, he thinks that he can love at times, and hate at other times. He also thinks that love can be bestowed on one, and yet remain itself although it is withheld from others. To believe these things of love is not to understand it.

This reminds me of an important line in Shakespeare's Sonnet #116: "Love is not love which alters when alteration finds." The Energy of Love is steadfast and unchanging, and available to all for applying to their life. It is "unchanged throughout" and bestowed upon everyone equally. It has no distinctions and is beyond the confines of judgments.

The Source is God and God is Life. The Energy of Life is Love and that Energy is whole and undivided. That Energy is in every breath we take, and in each connection we have with the physical world, and in all contacts we have with ourselves and other people. Our primary Loving Relationship is with this all-pervasive Energy we share with God and each other. This is the first and foremost Loving Relationship. God is Energy. When we are immersed in God we have all the Energy we need to Love, because we are immersed in the sacred Energy of Love. The end result of this immersion is Pure Joy. When you have absolute certainty in your awareness of Love, you must have Pure Joy. This is a law. The Yogis in India call this awareness Sat-Chit-Ananda.

❖ *Sat = Truth or Living, Lasting, Existing, Actual*

❖ *Chit = Perception, Understanding, Comprehension*
❖ *Ananda = Happiness, Joy, Sensual Pleasure, Pure Bliss*

And this awareness is the Presence of Love, the energy of God, the actuality of Heaven on earth. And what better function do we humans have on earth? To realize the truth of our own Being in the *Heart of God*? This is the primary "Loving Relationship" from which all others stem.

To answer the question, "What is your most important Loving Relationship?" we have to look toward the Source of our own Life, the Energy of Creation that makes our life possible in the first place. In India is a prevalent concept of the Divine Mother. God is not confined to an image of a bearded male patriarch in the clouds to whom we all must bow in fear and trepidation, so as to gain his approval and avoid his punishments. God is an Energy of Life that emerges as an Idea (Father) and manifests as a corresponding Form (Mother) through each Particular Entity or Element of this Creation (Son.) Herein is the Holy Family of the Trinity.

Love emerges as a Thought, an Idea, manifests as a Form, and individualizes as a Particular Entity. Light manifests as Fire and individualizes as a particular Entity, such as the Sun. The Sun is imbued with both Father and Mother Energy which is Love. This whole process we could call

GOD. Therefore, it makes sense to say "There is no Love but God's" That is like saying, "All that Is, Is, by virtue of its Is-ness." Love is all there is, and Love extends itself infinitely to create the Cosmos. Love is an action. Love is an Energy. Love is nothing in particular. Love is everything in particular. Love precedes Form. Love energizes Form. Love is the Invisible and the Visible, the Un-manifested and the Manifested. Love is Life and Life is Everything.

Our most important relationship in Life is to Love Itself. We have a responsibility to "remove the blocks to the awareness of Love's Presence" as Jesus helps us to do in *A Course in Miracles* through the action of forgiveness. Forgive yourself, forgive others, forgive everyone. Are we going to do it? Are we going to Love with all our hearts the Source of Love Itself? This is the challenge we have as individuals, and also the challenge we have as a human race. Will we continue to waste resources on the destructive powers of fear, or will we finally get sane and see ourselves as One. One humanity, under One God of LOVE, that is totally conflict-free and sane.

The decision is up to each of us to insist upon Loving Relationships. We are at a crossroads of human evolution. Never before could communications touch and reach so many. Facebook connects almost one third of the entire human population. Never have we had so much potential to put Love in the first place, over the ethers. Never before have we had the opportunity to grasp our connectedness rather than perpetuate our divisions.

This concludes *The New Loving Relationships Book*. Perhaps it will be the bible of a new earth that people carry in their satchels and purses while riding to work on the Metro or taking lunch in the park. We envision lovers reading it out loud in intimate moments together. Sunday mornings could be devoted to pondering a few pages in solitude, and going to the "church" inside yourself, the Heart of God, the Love of Life. This is your most important Loving Relationship, with your Self and your Creator, that is your inheritance, my inheritance, and everyone's inheritance that yields the Energy of perfect happiness that is God's true and only will for us.

LOVE,
Markus Ray—and Sondra Ray, who is my "Everything."

NOTES

NOTES

Made in the USA
Lexington, KY
29 July 2019